# The First Great Political Realist

# The First Great Political Realist

## *Kautilya and His* Arthashastra

Roger Boesche

LEXINGTON BOOKS
*Lanham • Boulder • New York • Oxford*

LEXINGTON BOOKS

Published in the United States of America
by Lexington Books
A Member of the Rowman & Littlefield Publishing Group
4501 Forbes Boulevard, Suite 200, Lanham, Maryland 20706

PO Box 317
Oxford
OX2 9RU, UK

Copyright © 2002 by Lexington Books
First paperback edition 2003

*All rights reserved.* No part of this publication may be reproduced, stored in a retrieval system, or transmitted in any form or by any means, electronic, mechanical, photocopying, recording, or otherwise, without the prior permission of the publisher.

British Library Cataloguing in Publication Information Available

The hardback edition of this book was previously cataloged by the Library of Congress as follows:

Boesche, Roger.
The first great political realist: Kautilya and his Arthashastra / Roger Boesche.
p. cm.
Includes bibliographical references and index.
ISBN 0-7391-0401-2 (Cloth: alk. paper)
0-7391-0607-4 (Pbk.: alk. paper)
1. Kauòtalya. Arthaâsâastra. 2. Political science—India—History—Early works to 1800. 3. State, The—Early works to 1800. 4. India—Politics and government—To 997. 5. India—Politics and government—997–1765. I. Title

JA84.14 B64 2002
320.1—dc21 2002005218

Printed in the United States of America

The paper used in this publication meets the minimum requirements of American National Standard for Information Sciences—Permanence of Paper for Printed Library Materials, ANSI/NISO Z39.48–1992.

"For without friends, no one would choose to live, though he had all other goods." – Aristotle

To my friends Mandy, Kelsey,
David, Eric, Heidi, Janine, Nina, Paula, Stephen.

# CONTENTS

# PREFACE

After completing my book *Theories of Tyranny: From Plato to Arendt* (1996), I found myself exhausted with the European tradition of political thought. I decided to revisit some old political theorist friends in Asia, specifically in China and India. Having written for some years about hard-nosed analysts of tyranny, I was impatient with political dreamers. "Don't tell me the world you'd like to see," I thought. "Tell me the realities of politics." Instead of Plato, Rousseau, and Hegel, give me Thucydides, Machiavelli, and Weber. And then I stumbled upon a thinker whose name and reputation rested deep and barely disturbed in my memory, indeed anxiously waving his hand like a schoolboy in class eager to be recognized, a political philosopher reputed to be the undisputed champion of all no-nonsense realists, a monster of cunning and bluntness. His name is Kautilya; he wrote his *Arthashastra,* or science of politics, about 300 B.C.E. He was like a chancellor to the emperor Chandragupta Maurya, who first unified the Indian subcontinent in empire.

Immediately, I encountered problems. Despite earnest and time-consuming efforts, I couldn't find a place to buy Kautilya's *Arthashastra* in the United States. I finally got hold of my first copy by having a student of mine mail me one he purchased in India! (If anyone reading this preface would like a copy of Kautilya's *Arthashastra*, contact South Asia Books, either at www.southasiabooks.com or by phoning 573-474-0116.) Even a recent Penguin Books English translation of Kautilya's *Arthashastra* was and still is available only in India. Apparently, those in the marketing departments at Penguin Books concluded that there was no American market. It was a reasonable conclusion. After searching for some years, I cannot find a single book written specifically about Kautilya published in the United States, Canada, or Australia. There are some older books published in Great Britain, and there is much material published in English in India. Nor could I find a single article published in the United States, although I have been told that there is one article, written in 1964, on Kautilya's theory of international relations in the *American Political Science Review*.

Why has Kautilya's brilliant book been so overlooked? First, along with major foundations, university and college faculties—more the former than the latter—help decide which academic fields are important and which are less important or which are of little importance at all. This changes slowly over time. In English departments, few were reading African-American or women authors several decades ago, and now priorities have changed dramatically. Before the 1980s and the upheavals in Central America, few scholars of Latin America knew much at all about Guatemala and Nicaragua, but suddenly world attention caused a shift in focus. Similarly, until the Palestinian voice, and Arab and Muslim voices in general, became louder in the 1970s, few political science departments had a specialist in Middle Eastern Studies, but now it is all quite common.

In the 1950s and the early 1960s, a number of American scholars were studying India, because India with its somewhat democratic institutions and its mixed economy—some capitalism and some state-controlled industry—was supposed to surpass communist China in economic development. In short, democratic India versus communist China was a Cold War lab experiment. As China developed more quickly and rapidly eclipsed India in such areas as life expectancy, lower rates of infant mortality, and literacy—but not of course in elections or human rights—interest in the Cold War contest faltered. As the world watched Mao's China lunge from the Great Leap Forward to the Great Proletarian Cultural Revolution, China suddenly became the focus of attention. Students of the sixties—my generation—who had been reading Gandhi, the *Bhagavad Gita*, and the *Upanishads*, surrendered these Indian writings and turned to the selected works of Mao, and, even more embarrassing in retrospect, Mao's little *Red Book*. With these developments in China, with the war in Vietnam, and with the economic success stories of Japan, South Korea, Taiwan, and Singapore, East and Southeast Asia have received almost all of the focus of American universities. South Asia—and Central Asia where the war in Afghanistan rages while I write this—has been woefully neglected in almost every discipline in the universities, although there are a few universities with admirable programs on South Asia.

There is probably one more reason. Demand from the public at large and eventually from students bubbles up and becomes slowly recognized in colleges and universities. Understandably, women, African-Americans, and Latinos want to read about their histories and about their cultural contributions to the United States. Similarly, Chinese, Japanese, and Korean immigrants have played a significant role in American history, particularly in the western United States, and the comparatively larger Chinese, Japanese, and Korean American populations have created a demand for courses on East Asian politics, history, and literature, as well as East Asian contributions to American culture and history. By contrast, there is no comparable demand from South Asian immigrant communities and families, because immigration from India and Pakistan—not to mention Bangladesh, Sri Lanka, and Nepal—is comparatively much smaller.

But the demand for scholarship on India is just around the corner. So, in a sense, this book is written for the near future when scholars take a fresh look at the rich traditions of religion, literature, philosophy, and political thought in ancient India. Why am I confident of this? First, India now has more than one billion people, and, within a couple of decades, will surpass the population of China. The most populous country in the world cannot continue to be ignored. Second, there is a renewed emphasis on adding to the study of European and American cultures the study of cultures from Africa, Asia, and Latin America. Already, more and more faculty members and students are realizing that literature today is not English literature, not even European literature, but instead world literature. Great novels are pouring out of Africa, Asia, and Latin America, and there is a profitable subindustry in finding the latest authors from India. Soon professors who teach political thought will have to know—because of pressure from students, other professors, and foundations—the traditions of political thought in China, India, Africa, and the Islamic world from Morocco to India. As the academic world moves toward multicultural curricula, there will be more of a demand for non-European political thought and textbooks and monographs to help with that. At that moment, in the not too distant future, Kautilya and his *Arthashastra* will be much better known. For you readers of the future, I hope this book is helpful.

Some of this book has appeared elsewhere or will soon. See "Kautilya's *Arthashastra*: A Pendulum Theory of History." *South Asian Studies* vol. 17, n.n. 2001: 1-6; "Moderate Machiavelli? Contrasting *The Prince* With Kautilya's *Arthashastra*." *Critical Horizons* vol. 2, no. 3, September, 2002, forthcoming; and "Kautilya's *Arthashastra*: War and Diplomacy in Ancient India." *Journal of Military Affairs,* forthcoming 2003.

There are many people to whom I am grateful. Charles Drekmeier of Stanford University first introduced me to Indian political thought several decades ago, and his book *Kingship and Community in Early India* remains important. The National Endowment for the Humanities provided me with a fellowship for parts of the academic year 1999-2000 to work on this project, and to them I offer sincere gratitude. My friends Sheldon Wolin and Peter Breiner helped me obtain that fellowship, and they had confidence that this project would work out. To them I give warm thanks. Occidental's Dean of Faculty, David Axeen, and my friend, Nina Gelbart, have been very encouraging and supportive. Michael Kerwin and John de La Fontaine of the Occidental College library have been of great assistance in finding articles and books for my research, the majority of which are from India and the vast majority of which I had to receive through interlibrary loan and document delivery. Former students Eroica Howard and Susan Lehrer acted with great energy and ingenuity to help find many books and articles. Mary Pullen and Cynthia Marugg have been invaluable in many details. Finally, and most importantly, I am not sure that I could have finished much of anything without my wife, Mandy, and my daughter, Kelsey.

Occidental College
Los Angeles
January, 2002

# INTRODUCTION

Kautilya's *Arthashastra*—to be exact in the spelling, *Arthaśāstra*—is one of the great books of political thought, but on each reader it leaves its mark, a chill as when a dark cloud blocks a warm sun. Is there any other book that talks so openly about when using violence is justified? When assassinating an enemy is useful? When killing domestic opponents is wise? How one uses secret agents? When one needs to sacrifice one's own secret agent? How the king can use women and children as spies and even assassins? When a nation should violate a treaty and invade its neighbor? Kautilya—and to my knowledge only Kautilya—addresses all those questions. In what cases must a king spy on his own people? How should a king test his ministers, even his own family members, to see if they are worthy of trust? When must a king kill a prince, his own son, who is heir to the throne? How does one protect a king from poison? What precautions must a king take against assassination by one's own wife? When is it appropriate to arrest a troublemaker on suspicion alone? When is torture justified? At some point, every reader wonders: Is there not one question that Kautilya found immoral, too terrible to ask in a book? No, not one. And this is what brings a frightful chill. But this is also why Kautilya was the first great, unrelenting political realist.

Midway through his *Prince*, in discussing how a prince should rule his subjects, Machiavelli wrote, "It appears to me more proper to go to the real truth of the matter than to its imagination; and many have imagined republics or principalities which have not been seen or known to exist in reality." (Machiavelli ch. 15, 56) This passage perfectly characterizes Machiavelli's approach to the study of politics. He was more interested in studying the way the political world is than how it ought to be, more fascinated with how the political world works than how it ought to work, more focused on the realities of politics than the ideals. Impatient with those like Plato, who dreamed up ideals to which the world should rush to bring itself into accord, Machiavelli was the quintessential political realist.

Some eighteen hundred years earlier in India, the first great political realist—Kautilya—was the chief advisor to Chandragupta Maurya, the king who united the Indian subcontinent in empire. Sometime around 300 B.C.E., Kautilya also wrote his *Arthashastra*—literally translated as a "science of wealth" but more often rendered as "science of politics"—that describes how a king should rule. In terms of offering frank and often brutal advice to a king, Kautilya makes Machiavelli seem mild. For example, whereas Machiavelli only examines cursorily the topic of assassination in the *Prince* and gives no advice about spies, arrest on suspicion, and torture, Kautilya discusses all these topics at length in his *Arthashastra*.

Actually, the categories of "realist" and "idealist" break down under close scrutiny. Surely Plato was the prototypical idealist, but he offered some lasting insights, indeed fine empirical insights, into the real worlds of democracy and tyranny in his *Republic*. And while Machiavelli is the most obvious realist in the European tradition of political thought, he had in fact his own ideal of the ancient Roman republic, an ideal that really existed in the past, as one can see by reading his *Discourses* or his *History of Florence*. In fact, when one reads Kautilya's *Arthashastra,* it is hard to know how much of the book is descriptive and how much is prescriptive, how much is real and how much ideal. We know from other contemporary sources that Kautilya was often describing the workings of the Mauryan Empire, but it is impossible to know in what passages of the *Arthashastra* exactly when he is describing rule by Chandragupta Maurya and when he is prescribing actions for an ideal king. In short, far from being sharp contrasts, the words *realist* and *idealist* give us a continuum of gradations between those more interested in analyzing the realities of the political world and those wishing to outline an ideal world toward which men and women can strive.

One must understand one more qualification of this supposed dichotomy between realists and idealists. It is false to believe that realists always advocate ruling over their subjects in a cruel and frightful manner whereas idealists wish to see humane and caring government. For example, Kautilya sought rule by a wise king, and he noted again and again that it was in the king's self-interest to be generous to the people, to establish something like a welfare state to provide work for all who needed it, to care for those unable to work, to keep taxes low, to provide for the public good by building roads and harbors and parks, and to discover grievances of the people and address them quickly. In short, social justice is in the king's self-interest, because fair treatment of the people prevents rebellions from within and lends to eager support of the king in case of an attack from without. Both Machiavelli and Kautilya judged political actions by results; the ends *sometimes* justify the means. They maintained that sometimes one needed to act in a traditionally evil manner to bring about the general good for one's people. By the same token, quite often acting in a socially just manner brings the best results.

*Realism* is a word more often used in the study of international relations than in trying to understand domestic policies. A much respected text on international relations gives four basic characteristics of a realist approach to foreign policy: (1) the assumption that human nature is aggressive; (2) the belief that international relations will always be characterized by conflict, especially war; (3) the emphasis on the military security of the state; and (4) the conviction that something like progress, which may be possible in domestic governance, is not possible in the international arena. (Jackson and Sørensen 1999, 68) Realists assume that each nation state seeks its own political, economic, and military interests, and in doing so, nations come into conflict and try to increase political, economic, and military power. Hans Morgenthau defined all politics as "a struggle for power." (Morgenthau 1985, 195) If each nation state is trying to maximize power—and this was Hobbes's view of the state of nature for individuals—then one must focus on making one's state powerful in order to avoid war, and hence realists talk in terms of balance of powers and countervailing powers. Kenneth Waltz, the very influential neo-realist, focuses on the structure of power or the constellation of interests in domestic policy—again, political, economic, and military interests—that explain why a nation's foreign policy doesn't differ dramatically no matter which leader or political party has power. Like other realists, Waltz also assumes that the world will always witness "the unregulated competition of states" and that success in foreign policy is "defined as preserving and strengthening the state." (Waltz 1979, 117)

Kautilya was also a realist in international relations, and as such, his foremost goal was to protect the state and its people. Kautilya certainly assumed that every state would act in its own self-interest, and he knew that one's own state must be strong—politically, economically, and militarily—to minimize the possibility of an attack. In short, he understood balance of power arguments long before anyone had invented the phrase "balance of power." In his own analyses of international relations, he put forward the now common view that a leader should assume that all neighboring states are enemies, whereas, by contrast, any state on the opposite side of a neighboring state is a potential ally. Or, the enemy of my enemy is my friend.

In one vital way, Kautilya differed from modern realists. Whereas modern realists are intent on defending the state and perhaps furthering its economic and military interests, Kautilya was an expansionist who wanted the kings he advised to be world conquerors who, he hoped, would pacify the population and bring spiritual and material prosperity to the Indian subcontinent. Thus, as much as any political thinker—more, even, than Machiavelli—he defended and encouraged imperialistic expansion and not merely defense of the state. Kautilya argued that at any given moment a kingdom is in a state of decline, stability, or advancement. While either in decline or in a condition of stability, each kingdom focuses on defending itself, making necessary alliances, and solving the internal problems—usually economic—causing difficulty. If, however, a kingdom has a prosperous economy, a well-treated populace, no calamities, and strong leadership, that kingdom is in a position to advance and conquer neighboring states. No moral qualms should restrain it from conquering. Kautilya makes very clear that promises made by a king or treaties duly negotiated and signed should not hinder invasion and conquest. Quite literally, Kautilya wanted a king who could shake hands on a peace treaty on Monday and attack on Tuesday. Trust, morality, and justice—such concepts play no role in international relations. However, sometimes, indeed quite often, humane considerations are in the self-interest of a conquering army. For example, one reads nowhere in Kautilya's *Arthashastra* of the army butchering ordinary soldiers of the enemy, much less the civilian population, whereas stories of this sort of slaughter were all too common in the ancient world. It is in the self-interest for conquering armies, Kautilya argued, to be humane and generous to defeated armies and citizens because, with such practices, a conquering king can recruit new soldiers, add new farmers, bring more cultivated farmland into his empire, and fatten the treasury. Needless to say, Kautilya insisted on killing the leaders of a conquered people.

One final introductory note. Who else might claim the title of "the first great political realist"? In the Chinese tradition, the great Legalist scholar Han Fei Tzu—whose writings were used by the King of Ch'in to unify China ruthlessly and establish the Ch'in dynasty—might well deserve consideration, but he was writing around 250 B.C.E., about fifty years after Kautilya. In the European tradition, admirers of Thucydides, and I am certainly one, might well argue that he is the first political realist, because he surely shows us the often brutal realities of domestic politics and international relations in *The Peloponnesian War*. The argument for Thucydides is a plausible one. Nevertheless, I favor Kautilya for two reasons. First, Thucydides' book is a work of history, and he did not write a systematic political treatise advising the leader of a great nation how to rule within the state and how to conduct foreign and military affairs outside one's borders.

Second, as many have pointed out, however well he described how nations interact, Thucydides did not discuss international relations in the absence of moral concerns such as justice. (Orwin 1994, 8-11, 117, 154-55, 201-2; Johnson 1993, 146-47; Riley 2000, 150) In some ways, he was as appalled as his readers at the brutalities engendered by foreign policies and warfare. While describing how the Athenians were justifying their empire to Sparta, Thucydides inserted a sentence that we would not find in Kautilya's *Arthashastra*. "Those who really deserve praise," says the Athenian speaker, "are the people who, while human enough to enjoy power, nevertheless pay more attention to justice than they are compelled to do by their situation." (Thucydides I, 76, 80) I interpret this to mean that Thucydides has an objective standard of justice, a moral yardstick by which to measure human actions. As I will show later, Kautilya has no moral standard by which to assess political action other than judging the good or bad results political action brings to the state and its people. Certainly Thucydides is some kind of political realist, but he too would have experienced that frightful chill if he had read the *Arthashastra*.

# Chapter 1

# HISTORICAL BACKGROUND

Kautilya's *Arthashastra* was one of the great political books of the ancient world.[1] Max Weber recognized this. "Truly radical 'Machiavellianism,' in the popular sense of that word," Weber said in his famous lecture "Politics as a Vocation," "is classically expressed in Indian literature in the *Arthashastra* of Kautilya (written long before the birth of Christ, ostensibly in the time of Chandragupta [Maurya]): compared to it, Machiavelli's *The Prince* is harmless." (Weber 1919, 220) Despite its importance as a classic of unsparing political realism, Kautilya's *Arthashastra* is little known outside of India.

This book seeks to introduce readers to Kautilya's social and political thought and tries to put Kautilya's political theory into the cultural and historical context of his times. Just as students of literature are exploring writings from around the world and not just English literature, so must political theorists understand that serious political thought has taken place beyond the borders of the United States and Europe. The reader who discovers Kautilya will find a political theory, which, taken as a whole, is unlike anything found in the West. For example, it is a theory of monarchy that must find a place for the key classes, castes, and subcastes of early Hinduism but allow for the supremacy of the monarch. Kautilya's *Arthashastra* also depicts a bureaucratic welfare state, in fact some kind of socialized monarchy, in which the central government administers the details of the economy for the common good, indeed, to some extent, on behalf of classes that had historically suffered. While watching Kautilya advise a monarch on how to balance the interests of Brahmin priests, powerful merchants, ambitious generals, and his own advisors, the reader is witnessing a timeless rendition, something like a virtuoso performance, by a genius of political realism. Kautilya's political thought, however, leaves no room for privacy and individual rights because Kautilya advocates a spy state, a system of surveillance, each watching each, that history has probably only found in the twentieth-century totalitarian states of the Soviet Union and China. In addition, Kautilya offers a work of genius in matters of foreign policy and warfare, including key principles of international relations from a realist perpsective and a discussion of when an army must use cruel violence and when it is more advantageous to be humane. We read Kautilya for the same reasons we read any brilliant political theorist: He makes us see the political world with new eyes, and he forces us to broaden our categories of political thinking.

## Historical Context

Kautilya was the key advisor to—and the genius of the strategy undertaken by—the king Chandragupta Maurya (c. 317-293 B.C.E.), who defeated the Nanda kings, stopped the advance of Alexander the Great's successors, and first united the Indian subcontinent in empire. Kautilya, sometimes called chancellor or prime minister to Chandragupta, composed his *Arthashastra,* or "science of politics," to tell a wise king how to defeat one's enemies and rule on behalf of the general good. He was not modest in his claims as to how much he helped Chandragupta. "This science has been composed by him [Kautilya], who in resentment, quickly regenerated the science and the weapon and [conquered] the earth that was under control of the Nanda kings." (Kautilya, *Arthashastra*, Book 15, Chapter 1, line 73, page 516; hereafter A.15.1.73, 516) Claiming only that he "regenerated" the *arthashastra*, Kautilya openly borrowed from previous works. One scholar counts at least eighteen precursors who worked on an *arthashastra*, and Kautilya mentioned fourteen of these in his work. (Singh 1993, 8-9) Some believe that other authors added to Kautilya's *Arthashastra*, even as late as 250 or 300 C.E. (Wolpert 1982, 57; Kulke and Rothermund 1991, 63) Kautilya's *Arthashastra* was very influential until the twelfth century C.E. when it disappeared, although it continued to be referred to afterwards.[2] The text reappeared rather miraculously in 1904 and was given to R. Swamasastry, the Librarian at the Mysore Government Oriental Library, who subsequently published it in 1909 and published an English translation in 1915. (Kosambi 1994, 142; Rangajaran 1992, 18-23; Bandyopadhyaya 1927, 16-17)

When Alexander the Great crossed the Indus river and formally entered India in 326 B.C.E., India was nominally ruled by one king, but actually divided and ruled badly by eight different sons with the name Nanda against whom there was great popular resentment. In short, the Nanda kings were despised because they were inept, immoral, extraordinarily greedy, cruel, and born as Shūdras, one of the lowest castes. (Bhargava 1996, 25, 34; Mookerji 1988, 6-8)

Legend has it that Kautilya, a Brahmin by birth, was insulted by a Nanda king, cursed that king, threatened to destroy him, and miraculously escaped disguised as an ascetic. (Mookerji 1988, 21) Afterwards he swore that he would destroy the Nanda kings and the Greek foreign invaders of India, and he wandered in search of someone who could help him fulfill his vow of revenge. (For examples of these legends, see Bhargava 1996, 121-28) In his travels, he came upon Chandragupta, who was from the Kshatriya, or warrior and ruler caste. Kautilya watched him as a young boy playing with others, and Chandragupta clearly demonstrated to his observer that he was a born leader. Kautilya immediately took him to his home town of Taxila, a famous center of learning at the time, not only in sciences and arts, but also in military strategy. (Mookerji 1988, 16-17) As Chandragupta studied and learned, he and Kautilya plotted and planned how to stop the Greeks, destroy the Nanda kings, and unite India. Justin and Plutarch both report that the young Chandragupta visited Alexander himself, who was often in or near Taxila, and somehow he offended Alexander, who ordered his execution—perhaps he offended Alexander by boldly telling him that Alexander could have taken all of India because the Nanda kings were "hated and despised" (Plutarch cited by Mookerji 1988, 6), perhaps by castigating Alexander for his tyranny (Bhargava 1996, 37), or perhaps just by his not so deferential tone of speech. (Raychaudhuri 1996b, 144)

The legends continue with the claim that Chandragupta and Kautilya raised an army with money, an interesting fact to remember when we see Kautilya stress the importance of the treasury, and tried to attack the heart of the Nanda empire, but were defeated. Several sources repeat a story that Chandragupta and Kautilya learned of their military mistake by overhearing a mother chastising a child for trying to eat hot bread from the middle, instead of eating the edges that were cooler. Allegedly learning from this comment, Chandragupta and Kautilya began attacking the "cooler" or more easily devoured outlying areas first and succeeded with something approaching what we would call guerilla warfare. (Bhargava 1996, 37, 117-21; Mookerji 1988, 33-34; Thapar 1996, 70-71)

Just after Alexander's death in 323 B.C.E., Chandragupta and Kautilya began their conquest by stopping the Greek invaders. In this effort they apparently assassinated two Greek governors, Nicanor and Philip, a strategy to keep in mind when I later examine Kautilya's approval of assassination. "The assassinations of the Greek governors," wrote Radha Kumud Mookerji, "are not to be looked upon as mere accidents or isolated events." (Mookerji

1988, 31, 28-33) By about 321 B.C.E., Chandragupta had taken the Punjab and Sindh from the Greeks, and by about 305 B.C.E., he had forced Alexander's successor in that area, Seleucus, into a humiliating treaty in which Seleucus married his daughter to Chandragupta, gave Chandragupta the territories of Afghanistan and Baluchistan, and only received 500 elephants in return. (Bhargava 1996, 38-41) (Some of these elephants, fascinatingly, made their way to Hasdrubal in Carthage! [Mookerji 1988, 37].) Between taking the Punjab and Sindh from the Greeks and concluding a treaty with Seleucus, Chandragupta and Kautilya succeeded in emancipating India from the tyranny of the hated Nandas (c. 317 B.C.E.), and, as a result, Chandragupta was and is now considered the first unifier of India and the first genuine emperor or king of India. (Bhattacharjee 1979, 143-48, 173; Bhargava 1996, 114) What accounts for his success?

First, Alexander's invasion succeeded in unifying a very divided India, and, in some ways, Alexander was as responsible for unifying India as much as Chandragupta. Second, Chandragupta and Kautilya successfully harnessed the popular energy of "the small republican states" (Mookerji 1988, 26) scattered over India, especially in the northwest. Whereas in an earlier period of Indian history, the country was "a vast rural democracy," (Mookerji 1988, 47) by the time of Alexander and Chandragupta, India had more "socially stratified republics." (Sharma 1991, 130; see also, Sastri 1996a, 173)[3] As Romila Thapar has stated, "In the transition from tribe to republic they lost the essential democratic pattern of the tribe but retained the idea of government through an assembly representing the tribe." (Thapar 1966, 50) These small republics put up a fierce resistance to Alexander's invasion, fighting what amounted to a people's war in which even women were used to fight. (Mookerji 1988, 22-26) Chandragupta could tap into this popular energy first to defeat the Greeks, and then to overcome the Nanda kings. After Chandragupta Maurya's conquest, these republican tribes were slowly "incorporated within the empire" until, by the reign of Chandragupta's grandson Aśoka (c. 268-232 B.C.E.), these republics were "completed amalgamated within the empire." (Thapar 1997, 122) Republican communities still existed, especially in the peripheries of the empire, until the Gupta empire of the fourth century C.E., and they supported anticaste movements such as Buddhism and Jainism, but ultimately the victory of the empire was a victory of a hierarchical caste system over a more egalitarian system of tribal republics. (Lal 1988, 20-23)

Third, Chandragupta built upon some of the unification of India by these very Nanda kings who, along with Alexander, "destroyed [some of] the small states and the petty principalities of northern India." (Bhargava 1996, 31) Fourth, the hatred and discontent fomented by the misrule of the Nandas made organizing a revolt that much easier. Chandragupta, by the way, made it impossible to return to the Nanda dynasty by exterminating the family of the Nandas, (Bhargava 1996, 39; Mookerji 1988, 35-36) something that Kautilya certainly would have advised. Finally, Chandragupta added to his own genius by relying on the advice of Kautilya, who had one of the great political and military minds of the ancient world and, in some versions, receives the most credit for unifying India. G. P. Singh, for example, describes Kautilya as the one "who overthrew the Nanda dynasty and installed Chandragupta Maurya on the throne." (Singh 1993, 9) Some of the *Purānas* give the entire credit for defeating the Nanda kings to the Brahmin Kautilya. (Raychaudhuri 1996b, 146) It is probably most accurate to describe Kautilya as an early Bismarck, a chancellor who helped Chandragupta unify India into empire. (Thapar 1978, 12)[4]

The Mauryan Empire established by Chandragupta and continued by his son Bindusara (c. 293-268 B.C.E.)—whom Kautilya also advised—and by his grandson Aśoka (c. 268-232 B.C.E.) was, and still is, astonishing. With a population of about 50 million people, the Mauryan Empire was geographically larger than the Mughal Empire 2000 years later and even larger than the British Empire in India, extending in fact all the way to the border of Persia and from Afghanistan to perhaps as far as Bengal. (Wolpert 1982, 59; Mookerji 1988, 2; Bhattacharjee 1979, 173; Ganguly 1994, 10-11; Rai 1992, 109) Bindusara and Aśoka extended the empire south, but they never conquered the very south of the Indian subcontinent, that is, Andhra and the land of the Tamils. (Bhargava 1996, 50) P. L. Bhargava has concluded that Chandragupta deserves to be called *cakravārtin*, which means something like "world conqueror" or "universal sovereign" over the known world of an extended India. (Bhargava 1996, 45-47; see also, Kohli 1995, 8, and Spellman 1964, 170-75) Tradition has it that late in his life Chandragupta abdicated the throne, became a wandering Jain ascetic, and starved himself slowly in the orthodox Jain manner. While it is plausible that he converted to Jainism, the rest of the story is unlikely. (Thapar 1997, 138)

Pliny—borrowing from Megasthenes, the ambassador from Seleucus to Chandragupta—wrote that Chandragupta's army totaled about 600,000 infantry, 30,000 calvary, 8000 chariots, and 9000 elephants. (Wolpert 1982, 59; Thapar 1966, 79) The administrative model for the Mauryan Empire, as it had been for Alexander's empire, was the Achaemenid empire in Persia (558-330 B.C.E.) founded by Cyrus the Great. Writing extensively about administration in his *Arthashastra*, Kautilya undoubtedly borrowed from Persian records and practices, and even Aśoka's famous edicts on rocks and pillars resemble, in style if not content, those of Darius the Great. (Thapar 1997, 127)

Chandragupta's capital was Pataliputra (near modern Patna), which he apparently seized from the Nandas sometime between 324 to 322 B.C.E. Pataliputra was probably the largest city in the world at that time, a city 8 miles long and a mile and a half wide, with 570 towers and 64 gates, all surrounded by a moat 600 feet wide and 45 feet deep that was used for defensive purposes and for dumping sewage. Pataliputra was surrounded by wooden walls—stone was very scarce—with slits to be used by archers. (Wolpert 1982, 58; Raychaudhuri 1996b, 158; Basham 1963, 350; Ghosh 1973, 66) These defenses are similar to those for Magadhapur as described in the *Mahābhārata* and for Ayodha as described in the *Rāmāyana* (Majumdar 1960, 35) Pataliputra itself "was about twice as large as Rome under Emperor Marcus Aurelius." (Kulke and Rothermund 1991, 60) The palace itself had a ground plan very similar to the palace in Persepolis, the Persian city built by Darius the Great. (Thapar 1997, 129)

Chandragupta Maurya consolidated an empire and passed it down intact to his son Bindusara, about whom we know little, and to his grandson Aśoka. Some argue that the extreme measures that we will see Kautilya advocate, and some of which surely Chandragupta must have employed, were necessary to bring order and the rule of law out of chaos. (Bhargava 1996, 102) M. V. Krishna Rao contends, "As a result of the progressive secularisation of society due to the innovations contemplated by [the *Arthashastra*] and the administration of Chandragupta, the country was prepared for the reception of the great moral transformation ushered in by Aśoka and his administration." (Rao 1958, 232) The unfication and pacification of India allowed the emergence of Aśoka, widely regarded as one of the finest kings in the history of the world. K. A. Nilakanta Sastri has written, in a fairly typical statement, "The reign of Aśoka forms the brightest page in the history of India." (Sastri 1996c, 202) Another historian has described Aśoka's rule as "the brightest chapter in human history," certainly an exaggeration, and labeled Aśoka himself as India's "philosopher king." (Bhattacharjee 1979, 177) This author also likened Aśoka to Solomon, which is not such a compliment if one knows the details of Solomon's oppressive rule. We must be careful in our conclusions, because as the historian Romila Thapar has rightly complained, sometimes Indian historians have glorified India's past to promote various nationalistic ideals. (Thapar 1978, 10)

Aśoka (c. 268-232 B.C.E.), whose name meant "sorrow free," was definitely an unusual and extraordinary king, and we know a lot about him and his rule because he has left about thirty-five edicts, mostly on pillars and rocks. Aśoka began his reign as an adherent of the Vedic religion—early Hinduism—and continued the practices of his grandfather and father before him, in particular the practice of extending the empire. Eight years after Aśoka took power, he invaded and conquered Kalinga, extending the Mauryan Empire south. We learn from a famous Rock Edict that he eventually suffered enormous remorse over the effects of this war—100,000 slain in battle and many more who died outside of battle, 150,000 men deported, and so on. Because of this, he turned toward Buddhism as a personal creed, took pilgrimages to holy places of Buddhism, and stopped his own killing of animals. (Sastri 1996c, 208-11)[5] Peter Harvey comments, "Aśoka gave Buddhism a central place in his empire, just as the Roman emperor Constantine did for Christianity," and he continues by noting that Aśoka was tolerant of all religions. (Harvey 1990, 76)[6]

Aśoka declared that in the future he would only conquer by morality or by *dhamma*—which is a Prakrit word often replaced by the more familiar Sanskrit word *dharma*—a word meaning right conduct, duty, religion, law, social justice, and responsibility. (See Dikshitar 1993, 240-59 for an excellent discussion of *dharma*; also Spellman 1964, 98; and Lipner 1994, 83-88) Romila Thapar has argued that Aśoka borrowed from both Hindu and Buddhist thought in formulating his concept of *dharma,* which was a practical and workable social ethic, (Thapar 1997, 149) and Sastri has written that, "The Dharma of Aśoka was thus a practical code of social ethics, and had little to with religion or theology as such." (Sastri 1996c, 240; Rhys Davids 1993, 292) Thapar has noted that Aśoka was trying to humanize the Hindu concept of *dharma,* or duty to the social order, but his *dharma* was an original ethic, not one simply borrowed from Buddhist doctrine. (Thapar 1997, 181) Nevertheless, *dharma* was his all-encompassing principle. In his first Pillar Edict, he announced, "For this is my principle: to protect through *Dhamma*, to administer affairs according to *Dhamma*, to please the people with *Dhamma*, to guard the empire with *Dhamma.*" (Thapar 1997, 174)

What prescriptions did Aśoka make in his wish to conquer the world by *dharma*? (Rai 1992, 114-26) Tolerance and respect for others, even those with different religions and backgrounds, or, as it says in the twelfth Rock Edict, "other sects ought to be duly honoured in every case" (Sastri 1996c, 235); love of the family; compassion, which includes respect for others, kindness toward slaves and prisoners, "reverence toward elders, and gentleness to animals" (Thapar 1997, 162); honesty; liberality toward relatives, friends, and neighbors; moderation and self-control, or as it says on the seventh Rock Edict, "but even one who practises great liberality but does not possess self-control, purity of mind, gratitude, and firm devotion, is very mean" (Sastri 1996c, 235); a system of social welfare, including medical centers for human beings and animals, the construction of roads for good communication, along with the digging of wells and the planting of trees for shade along these roads, and so on, all policies that he thought best carried out by the centralized administration of government (Thapar 1997, 70, 152, 180, 158); an unusual concern for the poor in rural areas, a concern that led him to tour the countryside frequently (Thapar 1997, 160-61); *ahimsā*, or non-violence, which sought to prohibit both the slaughter of animals for food and the sacrifice of animals. (Sastri 1996c, 237) "In time, the large royal household became completely vegetarian." (Harvey, 1990, 76) Interestingly, Aśoka did not condemn all war, but argued that when it was necessary, rulers should wage war with mercy and forgiveness; he also did not abolish capital punishment, probably a bow to the necessities of the time. (Thapar 1997, 168, 176) Aśoka sought not military conquest, but conquest by *dharma*, which involved the attempt to persuade through moral actions and words, and he helped in the spread of Buddhism by sending Buddhist missions throughout India from the Himalayas to Sri Lanka. He also took the unprecedented action of sending ambassadors of *dharma* to what we now call Syria, Egypt, Macedonia, Sri Lanka, Burma, and Thailand. (Thapar 1997, 46-90, 167-68; Harvey 1990, 77) Finally, Aśoka's concept of *dharma* promised not glory but happiness in this life for those who lived according to its principles, hinted at a Golden Age that might come, or even return, and suggested that a life according to *dharma* would lead to heaven (Thapar 1997, 163, 177, 155, 149). According to V. R. R. Dikshitar, in the sixth Rock Edict Aśoka said he was promoting *dharma* for "the common good of the world," and in the tenth Rock Edict, Aśoka stated plainly that he put forth the doctrine of *dharma* for "happiness in the next world." (Dikshitar 1993, 258)

As remarkable as Aśoka's reign was, Thapar is right in claiming that "the Mauryan centralized monarchy became a paternal despotism under Aśoka." (Thapar 1997, 95) Aśoka saw himself as a benevolent father taking care of his subjects, whom he referred to as children. "All men are my children," wrote Aśoka, "and just as I desire for my children that they should obtain welfare and happiness, both in this world and the next, so do I desire [the same] for all men." (Cited by Thapar 1997, 147) One can find this notion that the king should be like a father throughout Kautilya's *Arthashastra*. (Mookerji 1988, 59) Aśoka embraced paternalistic rule that sought obedient subjects and not active citizens. In the first Rock Edict, he wrote that "no assembly is to be held," by which he apparently meant festive meetings because he added that he saw evil in festive gatherings. Surely this also depoliticized the populace, and suppressing popular assemblies seems to go against the principle of toleration. (Thapar 1997, 150-52) Quite possibly his paternalism led to an administrative despotism in the name of *dharma*. (Thapar 1997, 174)

The Mauryan Empire collapsed rapidly after Aśoka; the centralized state designed by Chandragupta and Kautilya disappeared by about 180 B.C.E. In part this was because of weak kings who followed Aśoka, the division of the empire into two parts, and renewed invasions from the Greeks in the northwest. Some scholars have also suggested that Aśoka's pro-Buddhist policies and the pro-Jainist policies of his successors angered the Brahmin class and Hindus in general; others have argued that the much eulogized policy of *ahimsā*, or nonviolence, weakened the defenses of the empire; still others have suggested that the extensive tax policies of the government provoked considerable resentment; and finally, it is possible that Aśoka's prohibition of assemblies and his discouraging of the eating of meat created further resentment. In the end, the centralized government, especially in the absence of a true national identity, fell rather rapidly. Neither for the first nor the last time in the history of India, the village and its castes—not a centralized government—became primary. (Thapar 1997, 197-212; Rai 1992, 149-52; Lal 1988, 25)

## Reading Kautilya's *Arthashastra*

How should we read Kautilya's *Arthashastra*? Does his book describe the Mauryan Empire as it was, or was his book in large part a discussion of the way government ought to rule? The most careful historians understand this tension. Sastri warns us that Kautilya's *Arthashastra* is "a normative plan rather than a description of existing conditions" (Sastri 1996e, 178); Thapar claims that Kautilya's book "was not a detailed description of Mauryan administration, but rather a text-book on general administration" (Thapar 1997, 114); and Bhargava says the *Arthashastra* is "largely theoretical." (Bhargava 1996, 51) Despite such caveats and warnings, most historians conclude that Kautilya's *Arthashastra* is a reliable source that does somewhat describe the Mauryan Empire. Sastri acknowledges that the *Arthashastra* "expounds the principles and describes the machinery of [Mauryan] government" (Sastri 1996e, 189); Thapar maintains that Kautilya was "the theorist of the politico-economic basis of the Mauryan state" and "undoubtedly the general policy of the *Arthashastra* and that of the Mauryan state were very similar" (Thapar 1997, 56, 80); and Bhargava concludes that because Kautilya "became the prime minister of the empire, he must have implemented many of the ideas of his own book." (Bhargava 1996, 54)

Dikshitar notes that Kautilya's *Arthashastra*, unlike, for example, Plato's *Republic*, does not claim to be merely theoretical, but instead "there is an express statement by the author [Kautilya] in unequivocal terms that the treatise was composed for the use of [Chandragupta]." (Dikshitar 1993, 85) In the end, there is almost a consensus among historians that, as Radha Kumud Mookerji puts it, Kautilya's *Arthashastra* "is a picture of early conditions applicable to Mauryan India." (Mookerji 1988, 4) Burton Stein is one historian who disagrees, but his reasons are not convincing, because he mainly wonders how the wonderful humanitarian Aśoka could have emerged from the tyrannical Kautilya, (Stein 1998, 78) something I try to explain later in this book.

What evidence exists for such a claim? Fortunately, we have two main sources that corroborate the descriptions in the *Arthashastra*—the writings of the Greek ambassador Megasthenes and the inscriptions or edicts of Aśoka. Megasthenes was the ambassador from Seleucus to the court of Chandragupta after the treaty between the two rulers in 305 B.C.E. While he stayed at the capital of Pataliputra, he also seemed to know Kabul, the Punjab, and much of the rest of India very well. He wrote an entire treatise called the *Indika*, and, although the original work has disappeared, much of what he wrote was incorporated at length in the works of Diodorus, Plutarch, Justin, Strabo, Arrian, Pliny, and Appian. (See McCrindle 1960; see also, Sastri 1996d, 89-90, and Raychaudhuri 1996b, 135) Megasthenes confirms in some detail that Kautilya's *Arthashastra* is an accurate description of much of the Mauryan Empire, and we can see this in specific details such as the plan of Pataliputra, the description of the palace, the way the king held audiences, the details of the vast government bureaucracy, roads, shipping, irrigation, moats, the fact that Chandragupta was primarily guarded by women warriors, and so on. (Mookerji 1988, 143-48, 68, 58) In his introduction to N. N. Law's book on Kautilya, Mookerji outlines seven pages of similarities between Megasthenes and Kautilya. (Law 1914, xxxv-xlii) As Dikshitar contends, "there are so many remarkable coincidences [between the works of Megasthenes and Kautilya] while there are not very many appreciable differences." (Dikshitar 1993, 373)

So too do the Aśoka inscriptions—which are often descriptive of the Mauryan empire—corroborate what Kautilya says. Mookerji lists in two columns almost ten pages of similarities between Aśoka's edicts and pronouncements made in Kautilya's *Arthashastra*. (Mookerji 1988, 236-45) These parallels cover an astonishingly wide range of topics—the titles of offices and the protection of certain animals, the schedule of the king's day and the proper treatment of servants, help for the infirm and the avoidance of unjust imprisonment, and so on. Thapar concludes that Aśoka and his advisors knew of Kautilya's book and used it. (Thapar 1997, 9) And historians are correct, I am convinced, that Kautilya tells us a great deal about the Mauryan Empire, because, as Sastri states, "Megasthenes, Kautilya, and the Aśokan inscriptions, when correctly interpreted, supplement one another to a remarkable degree." (Sastri 1996e, 171) One scholar summed all this up well by saying that when Kautilya's *Arthashastra* was discovered in 1904 and published in 1908-1909 after being lost for hundreds of years, what was found was not merely a book but "a library of ancient India." (Basak 1967, 1-2) Because Megasthenes and the Aśokan edicts only confirm that many specifics in Kautilya's *Arthashastra*—but hardly the entire book—are descriptively accurate of the Mauryan polity, we must admit that we cannot tell exactly which parts of Kautilya are descriptive and which parts are prescriptive. Nevertheless, after a few caveats, historians of India really have no choice but to rely on the *Arthashastra* and assume that, used with caution, it offers a description of Mauryan India. (For examples, see Bhargava 1996, 90, and Mookerji 1988, 133-35)

Many Indian historians are proud to embrace Kautilya's *Arthashastra* as a practical book of rugged political realism—instead of the impotent idealism of, say, Plato—that actually helped to shape history. For example, D. D. Kosambi notes, "The Greeks make excellent reading; the Indian treatise [*Arthashastra*] worked infinitely better in practice for its own time and place." (Kosambi 1994, 141) Sharma maintains, "Kautilya furnishes us as full and complete definition of the state as was possible in ancient times. The Greek thinkers hardly discuss the constituent elements of the state." (Sharma 1991, 38) Somendra Lal Roy suggests that Kautilya was perhaps the first thinker to put forth "almost all the elements required to constitute a modern state." (Roy 1992, 98) An author named Indra sums up the views of many Indian authors: "The comparison between Kautilya and Machiavelli is not tenable. In in-tellectual acumen and in comprehensiveness of outlook, Kautilya is far superior to his Italian rival. Moreover, the Hindu author was a practical statesman, to whose guidance and advice, Chandragupta owed the foundation and consolidation of his empire, whereas the Florentine diplomat's experience was only of a few years in a subordinate department of the state." (Indra 1957, 95)

Kautilya's *Arthashastra* is thus a book of political realism, a book analyzing how the political world does work and not very often stating how it ought to work, a book that frequently discloses to a king what calculating and sometimes brutal measures he must carry out to preserve the state and the common good. One final question lurks in discussions of Kautilya. Were the harsh actions he often recommended necessary for the common good of India? Did Chandragupta and Bindusara have to act in a forceful and sometimes cruel fashion to defend India, bring order, and establish unity? (See, for example, Thapar 1987, 6, and Mookerji 1988, 51, 59) With the old order crumbling, with the Nanda kings having proved cruel and incompetent, with enemies on India's borders, and with the threat of anarchy within, weren't Kautilya's's harsh measures necessary, and haven't his critics failed "to note the nature of the times in which he lived"? (Saletore 1963, 51) In defense of Chandragupta and Kautilya, Bhargava says, "all kinds of means might have been considered necessary to restore peace with honor." (Bhargava 1996, 102) Put more bluntly, did India need the harsh measures of Kautilya the realist to render possible the rule of Chandragupta's grandson Aśoka the idealist?

## Notes

1. Despite this, one cannot buy this book through regular publishing channels in the United States. Moreover, I know of only one article (published in 1964) and not a single book published in the United States specifically on Kautilya and his *Arthashastra* (more precisely spelled *Arthaśāstra*). There are many sources published in English in India and a few in Great Britain.

I have used R. P. Kangle, *The Kautilīya Arthaśāstra*, 3 vols., 2nd ed. (New Delhi: Motilal Banarsidass Publishers, 1972). The first volume contains Kautilya's *Arthashastra* in Sanskrit, the second volume has a very literal translation of the *Arthashastra* in English with copious notes about possible alternative renderings, and the third volume offers Kangle's analysis. There is a more recent translation published and sold only in India by Penguin Books. (Kautilya, *The Arthashastra*, ed. and trans. L. N. Rangarajan [New Delhi: Penguin Books, 1992].) I consciously chose not to use this more recent translation because Rangarajan rearranged the text drastically and topically in the belief that this would make it easier for "the average reader," and also because Rangarajan admittedly departed from "literary exactness" to help out this imagined, average reader. (Rangarajan 1992, 24-25)

Two last notes for readers. First, I succeeded in obtaining the two translations of the *Arthashastra* (and several more books on ancient India) by contacting the import house, South Asia Books (www.southasiabooks.com). Finally, when doing computer searches about Kautilya's *Arthashastra*, one should be aware of much variety in spelling. For example, one should search both "arthashastra" and "arthasastra." Moreover, one must search "Kautilya," "Kautalya," "Kautiliya," and "Chanakya," all different names for Kautilya.

2. It is quite possible that some of the political ideas were passed on in some of the *Purānas*—especially the *Agni Purāna*—voluminous Hindu works, mostly written in the centuries after Christ, that supplement and complement the holy knowledge of the *Vedas* and talk of the origin of the universe, the gods, politics, history, rituals, and so on. (Rocher 1986, 135, 14-15, 197-98; Mishra 1965, 27, 37, 41, 54, 62-63, 72, 82, 176, 195, 204)

3. The best discussion of the history of ancient Indian republics is in Sharma 1991, Ch. 7-10, 87-141.

4. A. S. Panchapakesa Ayyar summarizes the legends of Chandragupta and Kautilya (7-40), and then offers an interesting historical novel about the two. (Ayyar 1951)

5. In an intriguing article, Israel Selvanayagam suggests that in the *Bhagavad Gita*, when Arjuna pauses before fighting because he does not want to kill, he is like Aśoka who gave up violence. In this, the *Bhagavad Gita*, which Selvanayagam dates to about 150 B.C.E., is a Hindu response to a Buddhist emphasis on nonviolence. (Selvanayagam 1992, 68-73)

6. For the most recent research on Aśoka's conversion to Buddhism and his relationship to the Buddhist order, see D. K. Ganguly 1994, 1-8.

# Chapter 2

# A SCIENCE OF POLITICS FOR A WISE KING

Kautilya assumed that the empire that he helped to establish would be good if it could be ruled by a powerful and wise king. John W. Spellman rightly notes that one cannot understand India's reverence and awe for the king if one does not grasp the Indian concept of *karma*. The doctrine of *karma* maintains that what happens to one in this life, both good and bad, is the result of actions taken either earlier in this life or more likely in one or more of many previous lives. (Sinari 1984, 14-19) One would naturally be in awe of a king because he must have done extraordinarily meritorious actions in previous lives. Says Spellman, "Just as the idea of *karma* enters so many aspects of Indian philosophy, we are not surprised to find it is an argument justifying the rulership of a king. The theory here is that my past lives and actions have made me what I am in this life. Since my *karma* was such that I am now king, I have, of course, every right to be king." (Spellman 1964, 12) The Hindu tradition generally regarded a king, once he was consecrated, as something approaching a god. (Flood 1996, 68)

Kautilya thought that a king was indispensable for an empire and that it was his job to advise a king about how to rule correctly. "For, the king, trained in the science, intent on the discipline of the subjects, enjoys the earth (alone) without sharing it with any (other) ruler, being devoted to the welfare of all beings." (A.1.5.17, 11) In the early pages of Book I, he is even more specific in maintaining that the king must uphold the system of class and caste, as well as the opportunity for individuals to pursue the four stages of life. "(The observance of) one's own special duty leads to heaven and to endless bliss. In case of its transgression, people would be exterminated through (the) mixture (of duties and castes). Therefore, the king should not allow the special duties of the (different) beings to be transgressed; for, ensuring adherence to (each one's) special duty, he finds joy after death as well as in this life." (A.1.3.14-16, 8-9) At the close of the *Arthashastra*, Kautilya reminded the king that he sometimes must use violence against the "unrighteous," if necessary for "protecting the four *varnas* [classes]." (A.14.1.1.1, 494)

## Classes and Castes

*Varna* is a word originally translated by the Portuguese as "caste," and even now occasionally translated that way, although "class" is a more appropriate rendering. The roots of the caste system extend back to at least 1200 B.C.E., and the four *varnas* were mentioned in the *Rig Veda* written approximately at that time. (Flood 1996, 37) "When they divided the Man, into how many parts did they apportion him? What do they call his mouth, his two arms and thighs and feet? His mouth became the Brahmin; his arms were made into the warrior, his thighs the people; and from his feet the servants were born." (*Rig Veda*, 31) *The Bhagavad Gita*, composed about 500 B.C.E., also outlines the four *varnas* or classes, and Krishna says, "all attain perfection when they find joy in their work." (*Bhagavad Gita,* 119) Most historians agree that sometime in the second millennium B.C.E., about 1500 B.C.E., Indo-European peoples migrated from some area between the Caucasus and southwestern Siberia (Azerbaijan? Uzbekistan? Kazakhstan?) through Afghanistan and into India, as well as Iran and, by another route of course, Europe. Calling themselves Aryans—*Ārya* meant "noble" or "free-born"—these people brought with them Sanskrit (an Indo-European language) and a polytheism that resembled Greek religion. (See Kosambi 1994, 72-95) Agni, the god of fire, is related to our word *ignite*; Dyaus Pitri, or "Sky father," is similar to Zeus for the Greeks and Jupiter for the Romans; the central Vedic god, Varuna, who guards the cosmic order, was similar to the Greek Ouranos and the Iranian god Ahura Mazda. (Hopkins 1971, 12) A warrior people, the Aryans conquered the Indus peoples, whose lives were devoted to agriculture and trade. "Except for the declining Indus system, the Aryans encountered no high cultures of the sort found across Iran to the west in Mesopotamia, Egypt, and Crete." (Hopkins 1971, 11, 10) Over time they conquered the indigenous peoples and imposed on them what Georges Dumézil has called a tripartite social structure—Brahmins, or those dealing with sacred knowledge; Kshatriyas, or those dealing with military force and protecting the country; and Vaishyas, or those dealing originally with agriculture and cattle rearing, but as time went on, they became involved more with trade, commerce, and the lending of money, and some Vaishyas became powerful land owners. (Smith 1994, 5-6; Das 1994, 147, 149)

The fourth *varna*, or the Shūdras, probably originated from "racial discrimination against these dark-skinned" indigenous people. (Kulke and Rothermund 1991, 42; Wolpert 1982, 25, 27; Thapar 1966, 38; Sharma 1990, 9-24) As Stanley Wolpert has written, "Acute color consciousness thus developed early during India's Aryan age and has since remained a significant factor in reinforcing the hierarchical social attitudes that are so deeply embedded in Indian civilization." (Wolpert 1982, 32) Originally, members of the indigenous population were called "*dāsas,*" or slaves, and gradually they took over the laboring part of society from the Vaishyas and became the Shūdras. (Smith 1994, 15; Lal 1988, 20) The Shūdras were not regarded, as were members of the upper three classes, as "twice-born" by religious rituals into full Aryan status, which is one clue that their origin was non-Aryan. Shūdras were excluded from the Vedic or religious sacrifice. (Smith 1994, 29) The life of a Shūdra was terribly hard. In the *Dharmasūtras*, or law codes written down roughly between 600 B.C.E. and 100 B.C.E., to kill a Shūdra brought the same penalty as to kill a mongoose or a peacock. (*Dharmasūtras,* 36) Again, in the *Dharmasūtras*, if a Shūdra killed a man, he was to be executed; if a Brahmin killed a man, he was to be blindfolded! (*Dharmasūtras,* 71) Later legal texts prescribed pouring molten lead into the ears of a Shūdra caught listening to the Vedas or holy texts (Wolpert 1982, 42); the *Laws of Manu*, an ancient text added to by many contributors but written out probably about 100 B.C.E., says that a Brahmin who kills a Shūdra should pay the same fine as he would for killing a dog. "If a man kills a cat or a mongoose, a blue jay, a frog, a dog, a lizard, an owl, or a crow, he should carry out the vow for killing a servant [Shūdra]." (*Laws of Manu,* 264) Just imagine the arrogance that must have accompanied the power and status of a Brahmin. When Kautilya considered a sizeable portion of Shūdras as Aryans, he was being somewhat of a revolutionary for his time. (Sharma 1991, 246) As Charles Drekmeier observes, "The author of the *Arthashastra* emerges as something of a champion of the Shūdras, espousing their rights as freeborn citizens, and going so far as to suggest that sons of slaves should enjoy the status of Aryans." (Drekmeier 1962, 198)

Eventually, another group emerged whose tasks were deemed so unclean that no one would want to touch them. These untouchables, or "outcastes," were not really a fifth class because they were considered outside the social order altogether. Thapar hypothesizes that the untouchables may have been "an aboriginal tribe, gradually edged away to the frontiers of areas of Aryan control." (Thapar 1966, 56; Sharma 1990, 145; *Laws of Manu,* 241) Untouchables lived outside the boundaries of town or village. By Gupta times (c. 400 C.E.), "like lepers in medieval Europe, [untouchables] were forced to strike a wooden clapper on entering a town, to warn the Aryans of their polluting approach." (Basham 1963, 146)

Kautilya outlined the "special duties" of the four *varnas*, and by his time these four classes had been the foundation of the social structure for hundreds of years. Indeed, ancient Indians divided the universe into *varnas*; they placed gods in each of the *varnas* and so too plants and animals. (Basu 1969, 9-10) As Brian K. Smith has observed, the categories of *varnas* allowed for classifying the universe. (Smith 1994, *passim*) At the top of the hierarchy was the Brahmin, a priest whose main tasks were "studying, teaching, performing sacrifices for self, officiating at other people's sacrifices." (A.1.3.5, 7) The job of the Brahmin priest was to study the *Vedas*—and the word *veda* means "knowledge" or "body of knowledge" (Hopkins 1971, 11)—the holy works that explain the origin of the universe, the nature of the gods, and how to carry out prayers and sacrifices. Said Kautilya, "The Sāmaveda, the Rgveda and the Yajurveda—these three are the three Vedas. (These three), the Atharaveveda and the Itihāsaveda are the Vedas." (A.1.3.1-2, 7) The Brahmin class brought to Hindu society an intellectual element; they were supposed to know both the sacred wisdom of the *Vedas* and the law codes. According to the codes of law in the *Yājñavalkya-Smrti*, "An assembly [for settling matters of doubt] is [formed by] four men who know the Vedas and [the treatises on] moral duty, or by a group of men who know the three Vedas. What that assembly teaches is law." (Goodall 1996, 296) A Brahmin who does not study and learn the *Vedas* is really less than a Brahmin. In the *Dharmasūtras*, we read: "Brahmins who are not learned, who do not teach, or who do not maintain the sacred fires become equal to [Shūdras]." (*Dharmasūtras,* 255) It is worth noting that women born into the Brahmin class could be scholars who taught the Vedas until about 300 B.C.E. and often priests who performed sacrifices until 500 B.C.E. In other words, at one time in early Hinduism, "women had an absolute equality with men in the eye of religion." (Altekar 1995, 338; see also, 11-6, 196-202, 338-41)

The Kshatriya, a warrior and/or ruler, had a special duty of "living by (the profession of) arms and protecting beings." (A.1.3.6, 7) Kshatriyas brought "heroic virtues" to society and a willingness to die in battle defending the social order. (Krishna 1996, 160) The Vaishya was generally a cultivator or trader or, as Kautilya put it, one who engaged in "agriculture, cattle-rearing and trade." (A.1.3.7, 7) Originally, Vaishyas took care of the pastures, but eventually they owned land, engaged in trade, and lent money. (Nagarajan 1992, vol. 1, 288-89) Vaishyas "gave primacy to the virtues of thrift, prudence, and the acquisition of wealth through trade and commerce. . . . The so-called capitalist societies are Vaishya societies *par excellence*." (Krishna 1996, 161) And finally, the Shūdras were generally either agricultural workers and day-laborers, or artisans such as tanners. As Kautilya maintained, the tasks of the Shūdras are, "service of the twice-born, engaging in an economic calling (viz., agriculture, cattle-rearing, and trade) and the profession of the artisan and the actor." (A.1.3.8, 8) Theirs was the realm of pure necessity, their jobs the ones that any society would just as soon replace by the efforts of animals or the workings of machines. (Krishna 1996, 162-63)

This hierarchy of *varnas* deserves several comments. First, it was unabashedly a class system, with its creators claiming that these classes were of divine origin, established by the heavens. Vivekanand Jha notes, "*Varna* was in essence exploitative in nature and content. There are crude statements to the effect that the Vaishya and the Shūdra are to be exploited for the advantage of the ruling class with the brahmana priest's active cooperation and help." (Jha 1991, 27) Smith comments correctly that "the Brahmins and the Kshatriyas can be regarded as united into a ruling class vis-à-vis the populace at large." (Smith 1994, 42; see also, Bhattacharya 1984, passim) Among other things, they did what all ruling classes have done; that is, they wrote the laws "for all the subcontinent." (Derrett 1973, 11) Nevertheless, there was great tension between the two classes with the Brahmins claiming a monopoly of sacred knowledge as well as the power to perform rituals and sacrifices, while the Kshatriyas wielded political and military force. The *Dharmasūtras* outline this alliance of the two classes. "There are in the world two who uphold the proper way of life—the king and the Brahmin deeply learned in the Vedas." (*Dharmasūtras*, 90) But class tensions also surface in the *Dharmasūtras*. "The king rules over all except Brahmins." (*Dharmasūtras,* 96) In the *Laws of Manu*, it says that what is best for kings is to fight the enemy, protect subjects, and engage in "obedience to priests [Brahmins]." (*Laws of Manu,* 137) Some of the law books had perhaps an exaggerated view of the power of Brahmin priests: The king "should not make priests angry, for when angry they could instantly destroy him, with all his army." (*Laws of Manu,* 230) And Brahmins, of course, crowned the king. (Basu 1969, 98-101; see also, Galey 1989, 143-45, 154)

Second, remembering that the entire system of classes was a hierarchy in someone's interests, we should conclude that the texts written down that justified the class system, that is, the texts claiming to be the divine words of the gods, were in fact composed by the dominant classes or interests. Writes Smith, "the fact that the *varna* system was in the interests of someone or some group who composed texts like these is not accidental but rather intentional." (Smith 1994, 82; see also, 4, 7) Third, the hierarchy is above all in terms of purity, with the Brahmins the most pure and the untouchables the most polluted. To signify this, and in keeping with the translation of the word *varna* as color, Brahmins were supposed to wear white, Kshatriyas yellow, Vaishyas red, and Shūdras black. (Stein 1998, 57) Kautilya provided the penalty of having one's tongue "rooted out" for one who "licks anything in a Brahmin's kitchen." (A.4.11.21, 285) If the shadow of an untouchable touched a Brahmin, not only did the untouchable suffer punishment, but the Brahmin had to undertake elaborate rituals—this fits Freud's theory of religion as public neurosis very well—to rid himself or herself of pollution. To take just one example from the *Dharmasūtras*, "as it is a sin to touch a Candāla [a certain kind of very "polluted" untouchable], so it is to speak to or look at one. These are the expiations for such offences: for touching, submerging completely in water." (*Dharmasūtras,* 45) (Some of the cleansing penances prescribed in the *Dharmasūtras* are astonishing. For example, if one speaks unintentionally to an outcaste or an untouchable, one must "remain standing" for an entire night reciting holy verses to the sun god. Also, to take just one of dozens of prescribed penances, "When a man eats barley gruel cooked in cow's urine together with liquid cowdung, curd, milk, and ghee, he is instantly freed from sin." [*Dharmasūtras*, 113, 239]) This fear of pollution led to elaborate rules governing all aspects of life. "What to eat and what not to eat, what to approach and what to shun, with whom to converse, share meals, and intermarry: such personal affairs are minutely regulated, with severe and exacting penalties for accidental as well as for intentional infringement." (Zimmer 1967, 151) Patrick Olivelle notes that the rules and practices about caste purity and impurity were, and are, intended "to sustain and reinforce" social structures, and that the anxiety caused by rules of purity "creates heightened attention to the boundaries that the rules are meant to uphold." (Olivelle 1998, 214) Finally, this hierarchy was not always rigidly fixed. Thapar notes that, whereas the Brahmins were always the top group in terms of status and the untouchables were the bottom class, "references to the intermediate groups often appear to be of a rather confused, if not a contradictory, kind." (Thapar 1978, 116; see also, Banerji 1993, 202)

While the class, or *varna,* of an individual was extremely important, for example, in matters of marriage (one almost always married within one's own class, although men of a higher class could marry women of a lower class [Deshpande 1993, 224]) and in patterns of eating (one must receive food from only those of the same or a higher class or individuals designated by the social order to serve food [Basham 1963, 148-49]), in fact the occupational group, subcaste, or *jāti*—indeed, *jāti* is the word used in India for "caste"—was, and still is, probably more important. (Interestingly, the

*Vedas* do not discuss *jātis* [Banerjea 1963, 74]; these subcastes emerged later with an economy requiring a greater specialization of labor. [Bhattacharya 1984, 3]) Thus, the system of *varnas,* or classes, was subdivided into hundreds, even thousands, of *jātis,* or castes, and as a consequence, one inherited, simply by birth, one's place in the vast system of division of labor. (Wolpert 1982, 42; Lal 1988, 23-24) For example, a child born into the subcaste of a miller (probably a Vaishya) or a washer of clothes (certainly an untouchable, because soiled clothes by their very nature are "unclean") was almost always fixed into that *jāti* for life.

Once more, it was a hierarchy based on one's level of purity or pollution. "Indian texts often explain the existence of the *jātis* as the result of interbreeding among the original four *varnas.*" (Smith 1994, 9) As a result, if the Brahmin is perfect, complete, and pure, everyone else is polluted to one degree or another. (Smith 1994, 32-34) Each *varna* has its own hierarchy based on occupational identity, although there is fluctuation and dispute among *jātis,* and even the untouchables formed their own subcastes so that almost every member of the untouchable class could think of himself or herself as superior to someone else. (Thapar 1978, 115; Basham 1963, 146) There was a very slow and difficult way for a *jāti* as a whole to move up in its hierarchy by means of the entire *jāti* adopting a new occupation that was in demand. Deepak Lal cites the example of silk weavers moving to another part of western India to attain higher status as "archers, soldiers, bards, and scholars." (Lal 1988, 24) One can imagine what modern urban and technological life does to the system of *jāti* when new occupations such as pilots and web page designers appear and old occupations such as typewriter cleaners fade away! It is worth noting that plants, animals, insects, and even celestial beings all belonged to different *jātis,* as if to underline that different *jātis* resemble different species. (Flood 1996, 59)

According to the early Hinduism reflected in Kautilya's *Arthashastra,* the kingdom will prosper, materially and morally, if each does the special duty outlined by *varna* (class) and *jāti* (caste or subcaste). "(The observance of) one's special duty leads to heaven and endless bliss. In case of its transgression, people would be exterminated through (the) mixture (of duties and castes)." Therefore, a king who ensures that all adhere to their special duties, will find "joy after death and in this life." (A.1.3.14-16, 8-9) One finds the same message in the *Bhagavad Gita,* that central book of Hindu philosophy: "And do thy duty, even if it be humble, rather than another's, even if it be great. To die in one's duty is life: to live in another's is death." (*Bhagavad Gita,* 59; see also, *Laws of Manu,* 246) In defending the system of class and caste, claimed Kautilya, the king assures "the right conduct of the world," (A.3.1.38, 194) and in this manner, the kingdom will prosper and not perish.

(A.1.3.17, 9) Certainly, Kautilya urged the king to use laws and force to protect the class and caste system. To take some examples, if a Shūdra struck a Brahmin, the judge should command that the Shūdra's hand be severed. If a Vaishya had sexual relations with a Brahmin woman, he would lose all his property, whereas a Shūdra committing the same crime would be burned alive. (A.3.19.8, 248; A.4.13.32, 290) By defending the established system of property distribution, Kautilya also upheld in this way the class structure. (A.8.3.27, 394) But by defending the right of Shūdras to join the army, and by saying that, "never shall an Ārya [including many Shūdras] be subjected to slavery," (Nagarajan 2 1992, 105-6) Kautilya was telling the king that it was advantageous to please and be just toward the lower classes. Says Jogiraj Basu, "It is amply evident from later Vedic texts that the subjects looked upon the ruling class as the feeder and themselves as the food." (Basu 1969, 116) Kautilya, as we will see, wanted the king and the state to combat such oppression.

One further point about the early Hindu society in which Kautilya lived: the goal of a devout Hindu, but not the chief goal of Kautilya, is apolitical or even antipolitical; the goal is *moksa*, or freedom, or, more precisely, release from the cycle of rebirth. In Hinduism, every living thing has a soul, or *ātman*, and according to actions in this life and previous lives, the soul wanders on through *samsāra,* which means rebirth or, literally, "passage." It says in the *Katha Upanishad*, "he who has not right understanding, is careless and never pure, reaches not the End of his journey; but wanders on from death to death." (*Upanishads,* 60)[1] The doctrine of *karma* suggests that how well one has lived one's previous life and lives, how well one has done one's *dharma,* or duty, determines what life one will have when the soul is reborn. (Hopkins 1971, 95-101; Perrett 1998, 63-66) The *Upanishads* explain the doctrine of *karma* in this way: "According as a man acts and walks in the path of life, so he becomes. He that does good becomes good; he that does evil becomes evil." (*Upanishads*, 140) One might be reborn in a lower caste, as a dog or a pig, or—as some Hindus believe—as an insect or a microorganism, or even as a plant. The *Laws of Manu* declare that a woman who has been unfaithful to her husband will be "reborn in the womb of a jackal [and] tormented by the diseases born of her evil." (*Laws of Manu,* 116) The *Laws of Manu* remind evildoers that because of past actions one can "fall into hell and [be] tortured in the house of Yama." (*Laws of Manu,* 123) The *Purānas*, written in the early centuries following Christ, outlined all sorts of terrible hells one could enter upon rebirth. (Lipner 1994, 231-34)

The goal of the devout Hindu was to end the cycle of rebirth, and Kautilya found this politically useful, precisely because this is such an apolitical goal. He urged the king to defend the four *varnas* "and the four stages of life" or *āśramas*. (A.1.3.4, 7; see Sharma 2000, 181-85) In Hinduism, the four stages of life are (1) the student who obeys, submits, and learns; (2) the householder who accumulates property, marries, and has children; (3) the forest dweller who leaves behind the things of this world; and (4) the wandering ascetic who foregoes an active life, eschews all possessions, gives up, in Kautilya's words, "all attachment to worldly ties," (A.1.3.12, 8) and, if all works out perfectly, attains *moksa,* or freedom. (Zimmer 1967, 155-60; Basham 1963, 159-79) In this idealized life, there is room, when one is a householder, for worldly power and possessions (*artha*) and for pleasure *(kāma,* as in the *Kāma Sūtra*), but the ultimate goal is for the soul or self (*ātman)* to end the cycle of rebirth (*samsāra*) through *moksa*. (It is worth asking if this life is in fact so full of suffering that one would want to end the cycle of rebirths. [Perrett 1998, 34-35]) As it says in the *Kena Upanishad,* "Those who follow wisdom pass beyond and, on leaving this world, become immortal." (*Upanishads,* 51)[2] Basham has summed this up well. "And with this transcendent knowledge came another realization—he was completely, utterly, free. He had found ultimate salvation, the final triumph of the soul. The ascetic who reached the goal of his quest was a conqueror above all conquerors. There was none greater than he in the whole universe." (Basham 1963, 247; see also, 244-55; and, Basham 1990, 36-50; Wolpert 1982, 44-48) Ramakant A. Sinari declares, "Indian sages have always thought that the domain of consciousness one attains in *moksa*, the delightful silence *moksa* generates, would constitute a cognitive state in which one absolutely transcends finitude and bondage." (Sinari 1984, 153) *Moksa* means "an unconditioned and absolutely static condition which knows nothing of time and space and upon which death has no hold; and because it is not only pure Being, but also pure consciousness and pure bliss, it must be analogous to life." (Zaehner 1966, 74) In classical Hindu thought, one can attain *moksa* by knowledge (*jñāna-yoga*), loving devotion to an incarnation of Brahman (*bhakti-yoga*), and/or by performing one's duties (*karma-yoga*). (Sharma 2000, 119-129)

This explains why Megasthenes, according to a fragment from Strabo, felt that Indian philosophers or ascetics were always talking of death and regarded death "as a birth into a real and happy life for the votaries of philosophy." (McCrindle 1960, 100) How far we are from Machiavelli's or the Greeks' love of military glory and political greatness! Nevertheless, Kautilya did not himself focus on *moksa*, although he certainly found it easier to rule if others did, because *moksa* for most Hindus was an apolitical or even antipolitical goal. Those who looked to the next life would not oppose a king in this life, and this sort of passage, found in the *Yājñavalkya-Smrti*, would only enhance the king's quest for worldly power. "Deluded is the man who searches for substance in human life, which is . . . like a bubble in water." (Goodall 1996, 332)[3] As R. P. Kangle points out, Kautilya was the first political thinker in the Indian tradition "to assign a high place to *artha* as against *dharma* and *kāma*." (Kangle 1992, 14, footnotes)

Because Kautilya opens his *Arthashastra* with the imperative that a king must protect the system of caste and class, it appears that he is offering a book defending the status quo. However, I will question this appearance as this chapter proceeds. I will try to show that Kautilya's highest aspiration was political, even heroic, greatness for the king, that Kautilya sought to use religion and any other of what he would call superstitions to attain this goal, that he regarded the state as superior to religion, that he did not acknowledge the supremacy of the Brahmins even though he was a Brahmin himself, that he wanted to use the state to break up the combined class power of Brahmins and Kshatriyas, that he insisted that a conquering army must include men who were Vaishyas and Shūdras, and that he found it useful for people to do the duties of class and caste as well as to seek liberation or release, because this depoliticized the mass of people when confronted by state power. In short, Kautilya readily gave way to customs and the rules of religion on minor issues of behavior and ritual, but he subtley promoted state power, the king's supremacy, over the demands of class and religion.

## Kautilya and His "Science of Politics"

Kangle translates the word *arthashastra* as "science of politics" (A.1.1.1, 1, and A.7.18.43, 384), a treatise to help a king in "the acquisition and protection of the earth." (A.1.1.1, 1) Others translate *arthashastra* in slightly different ways: Basham says it is a "treatise on polity" (Basham 1963, 51); Kosambi emphasizes the economic importance of the word in calling it a "science of material gain" (Kosambi 1994, 142); A. S. Altekar points out that *artha* literally means wealth or money so *arthashastra* should mean "the science of wealth" (Altekar 1962, 3); and Singh labels it a "science of polity." (Singh 1993, 7) I happen to prefer to translate *arthashastra* as a "science of political economy," but however one translates the word, Kautilya claimed to be putting forth what Heinrich Zimmer rightly calls "timeless laws of politics, economy, diplomacy, and war." (Zimmer 1967, 36)

The best European comparison is with Hobbes, who also tried to outline timeless laws by means of a science of politics. Hobbes claimed that there is a deductive science of the laws of nature, clear and self-evident rules ready to be discovered that are really more like mathematical "Conclusions or Theoremes." (Hobbes, Ch. 15) In the pursuit of a clear science, Kautilya and Hobbes have another similarity that I have not seen any commentator remark upon. Both thinkers believed the foundation of any science of politics must be clarity of language and crystal clear definitions of words, a model that Hobbes found in the deductive mathematics of Euclid. Hobbes maintained that we should start with speech and clear "Definitions of Words" and move to affirmations, syllogisms, conclusions, and "SCIENCE." "But if the first ground of such Discourse, be not definitions; or if the Definitions be not rightly joyned together into Syllogismes, then the End or Conclusion, is again OPINION, . . . though sometimes in absurd and senslesse words." (Hobbes, Ch. 7)

Kautilya was constantly doing something similar, not to mention two thousand years earlier, throughout his *Arthashastra*. In a crucial chapter on royal edicts, Kautilya stepped back to square one in his attempt to clarify words and sentences so that a king's edicts should communicate fully and leave no ambiguity. "A combination of letters is a word. . . . A collection of words is a sentence." (A.2.10.14, 20, 93) He then classified sentences. "'How is this so?' is query. 'Thus (it is)' is statement. 'Give (it to me)' is request. . . . 'Let this be done' is injunction." (A.2.10.27-29, 33, 94) At the very end of the book, he was still clarifying language: "A detailed statement is explanation.... 'One should behave in this manner,' is advice. . . . Setting forth the unknown (thing) with the help of the known is analogy. . . . That which, though not stated, follows as a matter of course is implication. . . . That which is applicable everywhere is invariable rule." (A.15.1.17, 19, 27, 29, 57, 513-15)

By clarifying language, Kautilya attempted to move forward into precise definitions. "Conferring benefits of money is making gifts. . . . Killing, tormenting and seizure of property constitute force." (A.2.10.54, 56, 96) In Book 3 of the *Arthashastra,* Kautilya carefully defined and outlined eight different kinds of marriage, (A.3.2.2-9, 196-97) although here he was clarify-ing tradition. Because he believed that one could not have a science of politics without clarity of language, over and over Kautilya tried to define matters rigorously. "Exchange of different kinds of grains at a different price is barter. Asking for grains from another source is begging. The same, intended to be returned, is borrowing." (A.2.15.5-7, 122) He attempted the same sort of definitions with political words. "Power is (possession) of strength. Success is (obtaining) happiness." (A.6.2.31-32, 319) In matters of foreign policy, "Entering into a treaty is peace. Doing injury is war." (A.7.1.6-7, 321) Hobbes tried to deduce from a few self-evident propositions a science of politics, and although Kautilya was not as rigorous and systematic as Hobbes, Kautilya was trying to do something very similar. In his science of politics, Kautilya was not like Machiavelli, who offered empirical and historical examples to support his insights and advice, but rather Kautilya tried to be clear, self-evident, and deductive in his claims. (Sil 1985, 111-12)

Because he was offering his readers a science with which they could master the world, Kautilya believed that a passive stance toward the world—for example, one who trusted in fate or relied on superstition—was outlandish. "One trusting in fate," noted Kautilya, "being devoid of human endeavor, perishes." (A.7.11.34, 358) His philosophy called for action, not resignation. "The object slips away from the foolish person, who continuously consults the stars; . . . what will the stars do?" (A.9.4.26, 419) In urging the king to rely on science and not the precepts of religion, Kautilya separated political thought from religious speculation. (See Sharma 1991, 265-66)

At times Kautilya suggested that he was giving his readers entrance into a world of secret knowledge that would bring enormous power and rewards, what he named "secret and occult practices." (A.9.1.13, 407) All of this culminates in Book Fourteen in which Kautilya enumerated fantastic secrets that could allegedly cause leprosy or cholera, make an iguana kill with its glance, turn a person white, allow someone to see at night, make another invisible, blind an enemy, and so on. "He should cause fright to the enemy with (these) evil, miraculous portents; because it is for the consolidation of the kingdom, a similar blameworthy conduct is recommended when there is a revolt." (A.14.2.45, 502; see also, A.14.1-14, 494-511)

As with Hobbes, the goal of science was power. "Power is (possession of) strength" (A.6.2.31, 319) and "strength changes the mind," (A.7.14.2, 366) which means that Kautilya's wish would be for power to control not only outward behavior, but also the thoughts of one's subjects and enemies. Probably his science could not promise all of that, but the power offered by this science was extensive. "An arrow, discharged by an archer, may kill one person or may not kill (even one); but intellect operated by a wise man would kill even children in the womb." (A.10.6.51, 453) Having as his first and primary goal to "destroy the enemies and protect his own people," (A.14.3.88, 509) the king certainly can do that with Kautilya's science. In fact, "he, who is well-versed in the science of politics, . . . plays, as he pleases, with kings tied by the chain of his intellect." (A.7.18.43-44, 384) Beyond protecting the kingdom, the king who uses Kautilya's science can bring to himself and his subject the three goods of life—"material gain, spiritual good and pleasures." (A.9.7.60, 431) As we will see later, wealth is the key to raising successful armies and having a peaceful and just kingdom, and Kautilya's science is a science that brings wealth. "The source of the livelihood of men is wealth, in other words, the earth inhabited by men. The science which is the means of the attainment and protection of that earth is the Science of Politics." (A.15.1.1-2, 512) In other words, Kautilya's book is the greatest weapon a king can have, and political science is more important than—or at least brings about—wealth, armies, and conquests. Similarly, Hobbes declared, "*Reason* is the *pace*; Encrease of *Science*, the *way*; and the benefit of man-kind, the *end*." (Hobbes, Ch. 5)

In the world of international politics, it is only "natural" that nations interact with each other through "dissension and force," and this is a typical argument by a political realist, that is, that there will always be conflict in international relations and, in effect, rule by the strongest. (A.9.7.68-69, 431) Kautilya was writing this at about the same time that Thucydides wrote *The Peloponnesian War* and the Sophists Callicles and Thrasymachus said to Plato that rule by the stronger was "natural." However, promising more than just political, economic, and military power, Kautilya assured his readers that those who follow his science of politics will receive spiritual goods and social justice. His science, Kautilya maintained, was for "the acquisition and protection of this world *and* of the next [my emphasis]." And his science also "brings into being and preserves spiritual good, material well-being and pleasures, and destroys spiritual evil, material loss and hatred." (A.15.1.71-72, 516) In fact, it is immoral and against social justice for a ruler to deviate from the laws and commands of this science of politics, and a king who goes against these laws "ruins the kingdom and himself with his injustice." (A.8.2.12, 391-92)

Kautilya, in the boldest of his promises, asserted that one who knows his science of politics can conquer the world. "But one possessed of personal qualities, though ruling over a small territory . . . conversant with (the science of) politics, does conquer the entire earth, never loses." (A.6.1.18, 317)[4] There is no humility here.[5] Kautilya's science brings an abundance of wealth and details correct strategies in politics and war, and with this science anyone can succeed. "And winning over and purchasing men of energy, those possessed of might, even women, children, lame and blind persons, have conquered the world." (A.9.1.9, 406) Nor did Kautilya see this conquest as something unjust. A king who carries out his duty, rules according to law, metes out only just punishment, applies the law equally "to his son and his enemy," and protects his subjects not only goes "to heaven" but "would conquer the earth up to its four ends." (A.3.1.41-43, 195) Whereas Kautilya did not talk of glory, I do believe he was thinking of something we might call "greatness," but this came only with social justice and the morally correct ordering of the world. "And after conquering the world, he should enjoy it divided into *varnas* and *āśramas* in accordance with his own duty." (A.13.4.62, 491)

Kautilya apparently meant by the phrase "conquering the earth" something like conquering up to what Indians regarded as the natural borders of India, from the Himalayas all the way south and from the Arabian Sea to the Bay of Bengal, although Kautilya said, "the region of the sovereign ruler extends northwards between the Himavat and the sea, one thousand *yojanas* [about 9000 miles!] in extent across." (A.9.1.18, 407) As Kangle puts it, in the Indian tradition, the world conqueror or *cakravārtin* was not one who conquered "regions beyond the borders of India." (Kangle 1992, 407, footnote; see also, Dikshitar 1987, 38-39; Raychaudhuri 1996b, 156; and Mahapatra 1995, 205; Indra 1957, 55) *Cakra* means wheel, and it is possible that the Indian concept of the world conqueror involves someone who rules as far as his chariots can roll, without obstacles or opposition. (Spellman 1964, 173) We know, however, that Mauryan India traded with Persia and China, (Saletore 1975, 53, 94-95; Asthana 1976, 214-18) but one finds no talk in Kautilya of conquering these lands. It is possible that Kautilya and the Mauryan kings did not regard those outside of these "natural" borders of India worth conquering, because they were "barbarians," or *mlecchas*, who did not speak a proper language and were hopelessly beyond culture or civilization. (Thapar 1978, 140-41; Banerji 1993, 36) One author quotes Manu as saying that beyond the borders of India was "the region of *mlecchas* or non-Aryans." (Indra 1957, 55) But then again, Alexander the Great, who must have been one of Kautilya's models, was happy to conquer and assimilate those whom earlier Greeks regarded as strangers or barbarians *(barbaros)*. At any rate, Dikshitar is correct in saying that this ideal of a world conqueror in ancient India led to an "imperialism" that was "one of the causes of chronic warfare," (Dikshitar 1987, 38), although the Mauryan dynasty did bring comparative peace for more than a century. As Narasingha Prosad Sil notes, "For Kautilya a world conquest is the true foundation for world peace." (Sil 1985, 123)

## How the King Rules

The king's first duty, just as it was for Hobbes's sovereign, is to "destroy the enemies and protect his own people." (A.14.3.88, 509) Similarly, he should protect the country from the "eight great calamities" which he lists as "fire, floods, disease, famine, rats, wild animals, serpents and evil spirits." (A.4.3.1-2, 262) Just as important, the king must protect his people from chaos within, a sort of Hobbesian state of war, or as Kautilya said, a condition when "the law of the fishes" applies, that is, when the big fish eat the little fish and all is violent turmoil, (A.1.13.5, 28; Mookerji 1988, 51) when there is no justice, the wicked prosper, there is no rain and no seed, fathers and husbands have no authority, women are raped, and dancing is no more. (Gonda 1956, 132) When the world was in violent chaos and "people ran about in all directions without fear," God gave the world kings to use force so as to bring order and justice. (*Laws of Manu,* 128) "If the king did not tirelessly inflict punishment on those who should be punished, the stronger would roast the weaker like fish on a spit. . . . (Everything) would be upside down." (*Laws of Manu,* 130) As Spellman puts it, "In ancient India, the fear of anarchy was almost pathological. Underlying every concept of kingship was the doctrine of *matsyanyaya*—the analogy of the big fish eating up the little fish. . . . Without understanding this idea, there can be no understanding of kingship in ancient India." (Spellman 1964, 4-5)[6] In early India, it was unthinkable for a sizeable territory not to have a king. "A people without a king is like a river without water." (Gonda 1956, 132) Says J. C. Heesterman, "the kingless country is by definition in an adharmic [without *dharma*] state of chaos." (Heesterman 1986, 1) In the *Bhagavad Gita,* Arjuna spells out this fear of chaos, and he includes a typical reference for the time that situates women as central to the moral order, unfortunately in this case the potential temptresses who can undermine it. "When unrighteous disorder prevails, the women sin and are impure; and when women are not pure, Krishna, there is disorder of caste, social confusion." (*Bhagavad Gita,* 47) Actually, the king's duty was to provide something more than just order, something called *yogakshema, yoga* meaning successful accomplishment of an object and *kshema* meaning peaceful and undisturbed enjoyment of the object. Roughly, *yogakshema* encompasses the overall spiritual, moral, and material well-being of the subjects, in short, the good life and not just mere life. (Chousalkar 1990, 10)

How to accomplish this goal of internal order? Most importantly, the king must uphold *dharma* (Gonda 1956, 53) and provide for the rule of law. "When all laws are perishing," wrote Kautilya, "the king here is the promulgator of laws, by virtue of his guarding the right conduct of the world consisting of the four *varnas* and four *āśramas*." (A.3.1.38, 194) Whereas it is best if a king can rely on well-established customary law, and Kautilya was willing to follow customary law in matters such as inheritance that have little political importance, (A.3.7.40, 216) the king must be willing to follow the science of politics and "the science of law" to issue royal edicts that override ordinary laws and customs. (A.3.1.44, 195) If the royal edict is in conflict with laws or customs, "there the edict shall prevail," (A.3.1.45, 196) which would give a king enormous power and was an astonishing departure from tradition. (For a contrary view, see Ghoshal 1952, 307-11) If custom was useful, he kept it; if custom could be finessed, he tried to; if custom must change, he overruled it. It is simply false to assert, "To [Kautilya] tradition is something sacred and inviolable, as to us even today. He bows to it with all humility." (Dikshitar 1927, 177)

Most important, laws must be clear, apply equally to all, and be backed by force. One can see this most clearly in Kautilya's discussions of how a king should use punishments, something Kautilya, following previous Hindu political thinkers, called the "rod" (*danda).* If a king can use the rod effectively and fairly, then he will achieve "the orderly maintenance of worldly life." (A.1.4.4, 9) In the Indian tradition, God gave the world kings to keep order, and God bestowed upon kings *danda* or the force of punishment. Says Spellman, "The only way that a man might be kept pure and righteous was by the fear of *danda*. . . In the absence of a king or when people do not fear *danda*, the inevitable result is anarchy and strife." (Spellman 1964, 108; see *Laws of Manu,* 129)[7] The parallel to Hobbes is striking. The state of nature for Hobbes was a "Warre of every man against every man," and to emerge from the state of nature humankind needs a "coercive Power" in order "to keep them all in awe." The government we agree to obey must have the means of violence, for "Covenants, without the Sword, are but Words, and of no strength to secure a man at all." (Hobbes, Ch. 14, 15, 17)

In the use of the rod, the king must find a middle way between being too harsh, and thus incurring hatred, and being too mild, and thus being despised. As with Machiavelli, incurring the hatred of the people is a disaster. "Being hated is a greater evil than humiliation," (A.8.3.16, 394) wrote Kautilya. "For, the (king), severe with the Rod, becomes a source of terror to beings. The (king), mild with the Rod, is despised. The (king), just with the Rod is honoured." (A.1.4.8-10, 10; see *Laws of Manu,* 129) All of this is similar to Machiavelli who warned constantly against being hated and despised. If the rod is used with justice and moderation, it brings to one's subjects "spiritual good, material well-being, and pleasure." If used unjustly, "whether in passion or anger," it "enrages" one's subjects. And, "if not used at all, it gives rise to the law of the fishes. For, the stronger swallows the weak in the absence of the wielder of the Rod." (A.1.4.11-14, 9; see Sharma 1991, 36)[8] It is extremely important that punishment be meted out fairly and equally and that no one be favored—an issue on which Kautilya is not consistent, because the higher castes generally receive lighter punishments than lower castes, a long established tradition that Kautilya could not possibly have overturned although he sought to mitigate the inequities. "For, it is punishment alone that guards this world and the other, when it is *evenly meted out by the king to his son and his enemy*, according to the offence." (A.3.1.42, 195; my emphasis) Similarly, a judge or magistrate should be impartial in assigning a punishment, "remaining neutral between the king and the subjects." (A.4.10.17-18, 283) Judges should be "impartial to all beings, worthy of trust and beloved of the people," (A.3.20.24, 253) although with Kautilya arguing for such a powerful king, it is hard to imagine judges with this much independence.

Just as there are punishments for those who do wrong, so there must be rewards for those who help the kingdom, and once more Kautilya reminds one of Hobbes who also wanted to use punishment and reward to guide people so that they acted for the general good. Kautilya wanted to reward those who did their jobs responsibly, those who were good informers, those who had key positions in state government and did not steal from the king, and anyone who improved, helped to defend, or beautified a village or the countryside. (A.2.9.9, 89; A.2.8.29, 88; A.2.9.36, 91; A.3.10.46, 226) In short, the king "should honour with favours the officer who confers great benefit (on the state)." (A.2.7.41, 85) In addition, "men are to be honoured on account of excellence in learning, intellect, valor, noble birth and deeds." (A.3.20.23, 253) If men and women seek rewards and fear punishment, then the entire kingdom should do its work smoothly bringing about the general good, all while individuals are motivated by a combination of self-interest and fear.

Because the king is vital to the smooth functioning of this kingdom, Kautilya advocated elaborate precautions to protect him. Interestingly, the women in his harem constitute the first and greatest danger to any king, but the king's last and most trustworthy protection should be, according to Kautilya, women armed with bows who are brought up just for such service and have no other loyalties to families or to caste. Thus, women are both threat and salvation. (Thomas 1964, 70) The king's bedroom should be defended by four different layers, something like concentric circles, of guards—armed women, eunuchs, dwarfs, and kinsmen. "When risen from the bed, he should be surrounded by female guards bearing bows, in the second hall by eunuch servants wearing robes and turbans, in the third by humpbacks, dwarfs and Kiratas, in the fourth by ministers, kinsmen, and door-keepers, lances in hand." (A.1.21.1, 51; see also, Mookerji 1988, 59-68; Dikshitar 1993, 108-111) Kautilya suggested elaborate precautions against assassination, especially by poison; the cook should taste the food "many times," and female slaves should not give the king garments without first putting "them to their eyes." (A.1.21.4, 14, 52-53) Kautilya advocated other precautions against outside enemies. "A rampart, a moat, and gates" should surround "the royal residence," (A.1.20.1, 48) the palace should have mazes, "concealed passages in walls," hidden staircases behind walls, "many subterranean passages," a safety exit hidden in a "hollow pillar," and so on. (A.11.20.2, 48) Similarly, the king shouldn't go into a park until "snake-catchers" have cleared it, and shouldn't go out into public space unless accompanied by a heavy guard of soldiers. (A.1.21.22, 27, 54)

What motivates the king? The king must be educated from childhood onward to control himself. "Control over the senses, which is motivated by training in the sciences, should be secured by giving up lust, anger, greed, pride, arrogance and foolhardiness." Indeed, a king who has no control over his senses and passions, "quickly perishes, though he be ruler right up to the four ends of the earth." (A.1.6.1,4, 12) Kautilya was a Brahmin, and Megasthenes noted that Brahmin priests maintained, "that all men are held in bondage, like prisoners of war, to their own innate enemies, the sensual appetites, gluttony, anger, joy, grief, longing, desire, and such like, while it is only the man who has triumphed over these enemies who goes to God." (McCrindle 1960, 122-23) The desires also ruined political decisions. Kautilya gave historical examples of disasters that befell kings whose desires rampaged uncontrolled—a king who perished, because he had "a sinful desire for a Brahmin maiden," another king who gave into anger and became hated, yet another king who yielded to greed and taxed the people severely once again bringing hatred, and so on. (A.1.6.5-7, 12) Like Plato's philosopher ruler, Kautilya's king must control his passions and desires. Similarly, the *Bhagavad Gita* refers to "the restless violence of the senses." (*Bhagavad Gita,* 53) The two passions a king must avoid most of all are lust and anger. "Lust means the favouring of evil persons, anger, the suppression of good persons. Because of the multitude of evils (resulting from them), both are held to be a calamity without end." (A.8.3.65, 396) Kautilya goes so far as to say that "anger and lust" are "the starting point of all calamities," and a king might learn to control them "by waiting upon elders." (A.8.3.66, 396) Of anger and lust, anger is "more serious," because "anger acts everywhere," by which Kautilya meant that it affects so many more people. "Mostly kings under the influence of anger are known to have been killed by risings among the subjects." (A.8.3.5-7, 393) Not only does control over one's senses lead to a moral life, it is also practical public policy. Just like Machiavelli, Kautilya warned against anger that can lead to violence against the people and make a king hated, which in turn can lead quite possibly to rebellion or revolt (*kopa*) by people treated unjustly (A.8.3.14-22, 394; Chousalkar 1990, 31-32) Like Plato, Kautilya believed that the people in general come to resemble their leaders. "What character [the king] has, that character the constituents come to have. . . . For, the king is in the place of their head." (A.8.1.17-18, 386; see Sil 1989, 44) Kautilya's ideal king must have a rigorous self-discipline. Indeed, no one in the kingdom worked harder than the king whose schedule prescribed by Kautilya allowed the king to sleep only four and a half hours each night. (Basham 1963, 90)

Although the king must learn to reign in his passions and senses, Kautilya did not advise him to forego pleasure, but rather urged him to enjoy pleasures in moderation. "[The king] should enjoy sensual pleasures without contravening his spiritual good and material well-being; he should not deprive himself of pleasures. . . . For, any one of (the three [goals of life], viz.,) spiritual good, material well-being and sensual pleasures, (if) excessively indulged in, does harm to itself as well as to the other two." (A.1.7.3, 5, 14) Not only did Kautilya assume the king would have a harem (A.1.20.21, 51) to provide him with sensual pleasures, but he also assumed a king would have such possessions as "carriages, riding animals, ornaments, dresses, women and houses." (A.5.6.44, 312) Pratap Chandra Chunder claims rightly that Kautilya held "that sensual pleasure should be enjoyed without conflicts with moral principles." (Chunder 1970, 30) Nevertheless, there is a parallel here between Kautilya and the Indian tradition and Plato. The *Laws of Manu* state that "a learned man" should try to restrain his desires that will invariably try to "run amok," and the wise man must become "like a charioteer (restraining his race-horses)." (*Laws of Manu,* 27) In his *Phaedrus*, Plato says that reason must be "the soul's pilot" who acts like a charioteer holding back, harnessing, and even channeling (sublimating?) spirit and desire. (Plato, 247c, 253c)

How does a king become educated so as to learn to control his senses and passions? We can get a glimpse of this in the education that Kautilya advises for a prince. Above all, a prince must learn "what conduces to spiritual and material good, not . . . what is spiritually and materially harmful." (A.1.17.33, 41) If the prince's teachers (who are also secret agents reporting to the king) discover that a prince might fall into one of these terrible addictions such as women or wine, they must construct situations that will lead the prince away from the desires of lust and drunkenness. "If in the exuberance of youth he were to entertain a longing for the wives of others, they should produce abhorrence in him through unclean women posing as noble ladies in lonely houses at night time. If he were to long for wine, they should frighten him with drugged liquor." (A.1.17.35-36, 41) This notion that women are a dangerous addiction, like gambling and drinking, was a common view in ancient India, one found for example in the *Brāhmanas*. (Shastri 1969, 78) In the end, a king should never put a son on the throne who is "undisciplined." (A.1.17.51, 43) Kautilya, as always, was strikingly blunt. If a prince cannot learn to overcome his passions and desires, if a prince cannot shake his addictions to women, wine, gambling, and so on, then for the good of the entire kingdom he must die. "If [a prince] is given up (as incorrigible), secret agents should kill him with weapon or poison." (A.1.18.14, 45)

Kautilya was not moralizing against sexual promiscuity or drunkenness, but rather he was making a practical and political judgment that such addictions can destroy the kingdom and the general good. "One doing whatever pleases him does not achieve anything. And he is the worst of them all." (A.7.11.35-36, 358) Kautilya apparently concluded that it does a kingdom no great harm if an ordinary farmer indulges in wine and women; a day or two wasted, and the farmer must return to work. But a king addicted to desire, as Plato said, can become a tyrant. "Indulgence in pleasures by the king afflicts (the subjects) through the seizure of what he pleases." (A.8.4.23, 398)

## The King as the All-Knowing and Caring Father

Kautilya wanted the subjects of the king to believe that the king is omnipresent and nearly omniscient, that his power resides in the actions of every state official, no matter how insignificant, and thus, breaking a law is in effect both rebellion and a personal assault on the king. To this end, Kautilya advised constructing scenarios to demonstrate the wide scope of the king's knowledge and power. For example, after a spy has learned that a thief stole even a trifle, he should declare that the king knew of this, and say, "this is the king's power." (A.4.5.14, 268) Upon catching thieves because of information from spies, a government official should make "a proclamation of the king's omniscience" among the people. (A.4.5.18, 268) To take another example, the king's spies should ascertain the size of an approaching caravan, and the king should inform the Collector of Customs that such a caravan is arriving, "in order to make his omniscience known." (A.2.21.27-28, 144) After the king has predicted that good things will happen to an individual or a family, then secret agents "should cause that (prophecy) of his to be fulfilled." (A.1.11.18, 23) Similarly, in foreign affairs or warfare, the king should use spies to gather information that it would seem impossible for him to know and strike "terror" in the enemy "by getting his omniscience and association with divinities proclaimed." (13.1.1-2, 474)

Whereas the king was supposed to be all-knowing, he was also supposed to be the loving father who took care of his subjects as if they were children, an ideal that one author calls "royal paternalism." (Bandyopadhyaya 1927,

64) Kautilya advocated something like a welfare state with the king as the kindly and caring paternal figure who "should favor the stricken (subjects) like a father." (A.4.3.43, 265) As we have seen, Chandragupta's grandson Aśoka carried this image of the king as father and the subjects as children to nearly despotic lengths. According to Kautilya, while the king himself, by means of his administration, should "maintain children, aged persons, and persons in distress when they are helpless," (A.2.1.26, 57) his judges throughout the kingdom should concern themselves with the affairs of "women, minors, old persons, sick persons, who are helpless [even] when these do not approach (the court)." (A.3.20.22, 253) Each judge was, in a sense, an extension of the king who was the final authority in judicial matters. (Sharma 1978, 125) Those who are poor and need help to support themselves should be given work. "And those women who do not stir out—those living separately, widows, crippled women, or maidens—who wish to earn their living, should be given work." (A.2.23.11, 147) Even after conquering an enemy, the king should "render help to the distressed, the helpless, and the diseased." (A.13.5.11, 492) Kautilya's paternalistic concern even extended to animals! For example, "(Horses) incapacitated for work by war, disease, or old age should receive food for maintenance." (A.2.30.27, 172)

To show the king's concern and to gather evidence, Kautilya insisted that the king be willing to hear grievances from his subjects in an audience hall, a practice probably carried out by Chandragupta and certainly one undertaken by Aśoka. "Arriving in the assembly hall, he should allow unrestricted entrance to those wishing to see him in connection with their affairs. For, a king difficult of access is made to do the reverse of what ought to be done and what ought not to be done, by those near him." (A.1.19.26-27, 47) This is thoroughly practical advice, because a king who is out of touch with his subjects—and we will see that Kautilya advocated the extensive use of spies to gather even more information—might find himself in the midst of an "insurrection" of his subjects and not even understand why. (A.1.19.28, 47) Even during wartime, Kautilya gave detailed instructions for building a camp that included an "audience-hall." (A.10.1.4, 433) Borrowing from Megasthenes, Strabo remarked that Chandragupta listened to grievances even while being massaged. "The king also leaves his palace not only in time of war, but also for the purpose of judging causes. He then remains in court for the whole day, without allowing the business to be interrupted, even though the hour arrives when he must needs attend to his person—that is, when he is to be rubbed with cylinders of wood." (McCrindle 1960, 70-71) This was probably not an innovation; even the *Dharmasūtras* assert that the king must build an "Audience Hall." (*Dharmasūtras,* 68) In the *Rāmāyana*,

King Dasartha was proud of his new Assembly Hall. "The King was always accessible, and fulfilled his duties as the ruler of Kosala without grudging the hours spent in public service." (*Rāmāyana,* 7) Aśoka stated in one of his edicts that those who keep him informed about the country should have access to him at all times, even if he was eating or in his harem. (Thapar 1997, 96)

Far from promoting justice for its own sake, Kautilya urged the king to ensure social justice and to establish a welfare state that cared for his people for practical and political reasons. "In the happiness of the subjects lies the happiness of the king and in what is beneficial to the subjects his own benefit." (A.1.19.34, 47) As U. Ghoshal puts it, Kautilya recognized that social justice is in the king's interest; for example, if the people are poor, they will become discontent and either support the enemy or slay the king. (Ghoshal 1923, 144-45) Kautilya himself argued in a long passage that social justice was usually in the king's political interest. If a king favors the wicked and discards the good, acts in an impious manner, punishes the good and rewards the evil, steals from and oppresses ordinary people, harms "principal men and [dishonours] those worthy of honour," then he will create only greed and disaffection among the people. "Subjects, when impoverished, become greedy; when greedy they become disaffected; when disaffected they either go over to the enemy or themselves kill the master." (7.5.19-27, 335) As S. N. Singh comments, "in his own interest the king had to do good to the people as on this basis alone he could himself be happy and prosperous. Possessed of subjects who are indifferent to the king's interests, the king was easily overpowered by his enemy." (Singh 1992, 149) To show that social justice, or rule by dharma, is often in the king's best interest is a far cry from claiming Kautilya to be an idealist, as does one scholar. (Sil 1984, 21)

This is part of Kautilya's answer to those who consider him immoral. In so many cases, the moral or just action is also in the self-interest of the ruler or, to put it in another way, the right action often leads to the general good. Thus, when T. W. Rhys Davies calls Kautilya "depraved at heart" and "not so much immoral as unmoral" (Rhys Davids 1993, 270), and when Erich Frauwallner says that Kautilya had "no moral scruples" (Frauwallner 2 1993, 216) when it came to political action, they are offering a shallow reading of the *Arthashastra* and not recognizing how often the morally correct action is in fact in the king's self-interest. In the next section, we will see that even when Kautilya defended the use of spies and assassination, he did not do so in the absence of moral justification.

## Notes

1. In Greek philosophy, Pythagoras (c. 570-530 B.C.E.) quite likely encountered Indian philosophy and the doctrine of transmigration or reincarnation of souls in either Babylonia or Egypt. (Robinson 1968, 57, 61; Clarke 1997, 37). Plato borrowed this doctrine of the transmigration of souls from the Pythagoreans of his own time, and we find it in Book 10 of his *Republic.*

2. The implicit argument or assumption in this idea of *moksa* or release is that this world is full of suffering, a claim made much more explicit by the Buddha. One can see this claim also in a passage from the *Laws of Manu.* "The man who has the ability to see correctly is not bound by the effects of his past actions, but the man who lacks this vision is caught up in the cycle of transmigration. . . . He should abandon this foul-smelling, tormented, impermanent dwelling-place of living beings, filled with urine and excrement, pervaded by old age and sorrow, infested by illness, and polluted by passion." (*Laws of Manu,* 124)

3. G. C. Pande says, "The Vedic search for the spirit did not deny the world. It rather accepted the world as a gift and expression of a divine reality. . . . As a practical consequence the Upanishadic quest seeks to go beyond the life of worldliness and ritualism centred in action but does not usually advocate the radical renunciation of all life of action. Nor does it condemn the world as a vale of tears although it recognizes the unsatisfactory character of worldly goods and gains and stresses the need for spiritual enlightenment for realising that Bliss is the essence of being." (Pande 1984, 60)

4. Rajendra Prasad is just wrong in concluding that Kautilya favored a kingdom of "small size." (Prasad 1989, 95)

5. Contrast Kautilya's swagger with this passage. "[The king] should learn humility from [Brahmins] even if he is always humble, for the king who is humble is never destroyed." (*Laws of Manu,* 132)

6. Contrast this with Hobbes's understanding of the state of nature as a state of war, and notice how Hobbes assumed a more commercial and economically advanced society that would be lost if humankind returned to a state of war. "Hereby it is manifest, that during the time men live without a common Power to keep them all in awe, they are in a condition which is called Warre; and such a warre, as if of every man, against every man. . . . In such condition, there is no place for Industry; because the fruit thereof is uncertain; and consequently no Culture of the Earth; no Navigation, nor use

of the commodities that may be imported by Sea; no commodious Building; no Instruments of moving, and removing such things as require much force; no Knowledge of the face of the earth; no account of Time; no Arts; no Letters; no Society; and which is worst of all, continuall feare, and danger of violent death; And the life of man, solitary, poore, nasty, brutish, and short." (Hobbes, Ch. 13)

7. "The whole universe trembles before (a king) whose rod is constantly erect; he should therefore subjugate all living beings by that very rod." (*Laws of Manu,* 139) "If there be no Power erected, or not great enough for our security; every man will and may lawfully rely on his own strength and art." (Hobbes, Ch. 17)

8. Kautilya had a commendable record in trying to protect women from domestic violence and violence in general. The magistrates "shall impale on the stake those who beat a man or a woman with force." (A.4.11.7, 283). See also, A.3.3.8-9, 202; A.3.3.26, 204. For the subject of violence against women, see Bhattacharji 1994, 158-64.

# Chapter 3

## KAUTILYA'S SPY STATE

Kautilya described a kingdom in which every subject would be spied upon constantly, starting with the king's highest ministers. As we will see later, Kautilya thought that a king would require an enormous and elaborate bureaucracy, but for now we note only that Kautilya recognized that a king needs ministers. "Rulership can be successfully carried out (only) with the help of associates. One wheel alone does not turn. Therefore, he should appoint ministers and listen to their [opinions]." (A.1.7.9, 14) A king should have, according to Kautilya, three or four chief ministers; one chief minister would do as he pleased, and two chief ministers could unite against the king. (A.1.15.33-38, 34) Kautilya acknowledged that serving an excellent king as an advisor was an extremely honorable occupation. In a passage perhaps describing himself, Kautilya noted that, "One, conversant with the ways of the world, should seek service with a king, endowed with personal excellences." (A.5.4.1, 305) While Kautilya knew that being an advisor was an important occupation, he also knew that it was difficult and dangerous. Sometimes an advisor must try to correct a badly behaved king, sometimes a minister must retire from service, sometimes one must save oneself and serve an allied state, and once in a while a minister must engineer calamity for the king and promote a crown prince to the throne. (A.5.5.12-14, 309; A.5.6.18, 311) "For, self-protection must always be first secured by the wise (person), for the conduct of those serving a king has been stated to be like (remaining) in fire." (A.5.4.16, 307)

Because Kautilya regarded ministers as dangerous, he insisted that they must constantly be tested. "After appointing ministers. . . . [the king] should test their integrity by means of secret tests." (A.1.10.1, 18) Kautilya advocated four tests: the test of piety, the test of material gain, the test of lust, and the test of fear. In each case, Kautilya sought to contrive temptations—by saying the king is impious, or by offering a huge bribe, or by telling a minister that the queen is in love with him, or by jailing a minister falsely and trying to incite him to treason—to test a minister's loyalty. In general, those who failed such tests were to work in mines, factories, or forests. (A.1.10.1-20, 18-21) (Apparently, however, one who failed the test of lust and slept with the queen would die painfully. "For having relations with the king's wife, the [punishment] in all cases [shall be] cooking in a big jar." [A.4.13.33, 290]) In similar ways, Kautilya urged kings to test judges, village chiefs, and departmental heads. (A.4.4.6-9, 265-66)

Spying went well beyond tempting ministers. "When [the king] has set spies on the high officials," Kautilya insisted, "he should set spies on the citizens and the country people." (A.1.13.1, 28) The list of possible spies is overwhelming. "The Administrator should station in the country (secret agents) appearing as holy ascetics, wandering monks, cart-drivers, wandering minstrels, jugglers, tramps, fortune-tellers, soothsayers, astrologers, physicians, lunatics, dumb persons, deaf persons, vintners, dealers in bread, dealers in cooked meat, and dealers in cooked rice." (A.4.4.3, 265) Kautilya sought spies who would test and ascertain the loyalty of farmers and of soldiers, of heads of departments and of all officials in the government's bureaucracy, and he implied that there would be frequent surprise inspections. (A.2.35.13, 184; A.5.3.47, 305; A.2.7.9, 82; A.2.9.2, 89) Kautilya wanted secret agents who would spy on both enemies and allies, and he would secure the loyalty of double agents by "taking charge of their sons and wives." (A.1.12.19, 20, 26) He showed no hesitation in using women and children as spies and, even, as assassins. (A.12.4.9-10, 468)[1]

Kautilya was frightfully detailed and thorough. Of minor officials who must handle money and valuables, Kautilya said, "of those (officers) the ways of embezzlement are forty," and he set about listing these forty ways and how one might nonetheless catch an embezzler. (A.2.8.20, 21-25, 86-88) He admitted that one can never be entirely certain that those who deal with the king's money, gold, or other valuables haven't taken something. "Just as fish moving inside water cannot be known when drinking water, even so officers appointed for carrying out works [related to valuables] cannot be known when appropriating money. It is possible to know even the path of birds flying in the sky, but not the ways of officers moving with their intentions concealed." (A.2.9.33-34, 91) Nevertheless, Kautilya sought to prevent embezzlement. For example, artisans who work with gold "shall enter and leave [the workplace] after their garments, hands and private parts are searched." (A.2.13.33, 113)

Because of this massive use of spying, Kautilya's kingdom was a police state, and anyone who did anything unusual was watched and generally arrested. For example, not only should the king build alehouses to regulate and watch those who drink alcohol, but he should also use those alehouses to spy. Secret agents should "ascertain the normal and occasional expenditures (of customers) and get information about strangers," and "female slaves of beautiful appearance" should find out all they can about strangers and locals when they are drunk and/or asleep. (A.2.25.12,15,11-15, 154) While spies should "report one who spends lavishly and one who does a rash deed," they should also discover and report one who has had a wound treated secretly and anyone who has committed "an unwholesome act." (A.2.36.9-10, 185) The *Laws of Manu*, written down after Kautilya's *Arthashastra*, describes in considerable detail—and certainly endorses—this kind of spying that led to arrest on suspicion and even incitement to crime so wrongdoers could be caught. (*Laws of Manu,* 225-26)

Those who defend Kautilya's use of spies regard these informers as no more than experts who gather public opinion and report it to the king, just as do modern public opinion pollsters. By using spies, a king could keep in touch with public sentiment and be aware early of any grievances. Megasthenes noted that these spies discovered what was going on in the kingdom; as Arrian detailed, these spies "report everything to the king," and it is illegal "for these to give a false report—but indeed no Indian is accused of lying." (McCrindle 1960, 217-18) (Strabo, another who borrowed his information from Megasthenes, declared that a person convicted "of bearing false witness" had his hands and feet cut off. [McCrindle 1960, 70]) One of Aśoka's inscriptions also notes that he used officers, to whom he gave free access day and night, just to report what was happening in the country. (Cited by Mookerji 1988, 121) King Dhritarāshtra in the *Mahābhārata*, "constantly enquired of his spies, 'What are people talking about?'" (*Mahābhārata*, 40) Bhargava states that under Chandragupta Maurya, "the spies were employed not only to detect criminals, but also to get information about the views of the people." (Bhargava 1996, 63; see *Laws of Manu,* 229) Mookerji and Bhargava are certainly correct that spies did report public opinion both within the kingdom and in foreign countries (see A.1.16, 36-39), but even if we acknowledge that spies fulfilled this valuable function of taking the pulse of the people, the kingdom that Kautilya wished for was still a police state, and scholars who focus only on how spies reported public opinion are merely putting forth apologetics for Kautilya.

## Arrest on Suspicion

Because there is no language in Kautilya's *Arthashastra* that speaks to the rights of the individual, Kautilya readily sanctioned arrest on suspicion. Among the many varieties of people that he suggested the police arrest on suspicion are "one with a small wage"; one falsely declaring his name or occupation; "one addicted to meat, wine, [or] eating of food"; "one who spends lavishly"; "one addicted to prostitutes"; "one travelling frequently"; "one moving at an odd time in a solitary place"; "one always staying inside the house"; "one devoted to a beloved"; one moving "stealthily" in the shadows of walls at night; "one who entertains a feeling of hostility"; one who has committed a previous offense; one who becomes anxious when he sees an official; and so on. After considerably more than a half page paragraph, Kautilya stated, "Thus ends (the topic) of arrest on suspicion." (A.4.6.1-2, 268-69; see also, A.2.36.34-38, 188) In regard to people "suspected of treason," Kautilya did not hesitate to list many ways in which one could entrap them. (A.5.2.52-70, 300-301)

Apparently, Kautilya did want to institute judicial protection for the individual. Having declared that magistrates should remain "neutral between the king and the subjects," Kautilya wanted judges who could be "impartial to all beings, worthy of trust and beloved of the people," (A. 4.10.17-18, 283; A.3.20.24, 253) although it is hard to imagine judges being impartial in the face of such enormous power wielded by the king and the state. Also, Kautilya did not seem to trust a single report of one spy, but instead wanted independent corroboration of suspicious or illegal activity. "When there is agreement in the reports of three (spies), credence (should be given)." (A.1.12.15, 26) Kautilya also prescribed a hefty fine "in case punishment is inflicted on those not deserving to be punished." (A.4.13.42, 291)

Nor did the *Arthashastra* allow for a right to privacy; indeed, Kautilya wanted the state to regulate the smallest and most intimate acts. For example, "If a man and a woman, with sexual intercourse in view, indulge in gestures with limbs or indecent conversation in secret," the authorities will fine them. (A.3.3.25, 203) Or again, "A wife disliking her husband (and) not adorning herself (for fulfillment of marital duty) during seven menstrual periods" must consent to having her husband have sex with another woman. (A.3.3.12, 202) No country that I have ever heard of sought to intrude in these ways into even the most minor of undertakings of everyday life. To take another example, "Washermen shall wash garments on wooden boards or smooth slabs of stone," or they will face a fine. (A.4.1.14-15, 255) One begins to wonder if there are no other satisfactory ways to wash clothes and if one must ask the police if a particular stone is smooth enough!

Kautilya sought to curtail severely what we would call the right to free speech. "A person deserves the lowest fine (for violence)," he wrote, "for reviling his own country and village, the middle fine for reviling his own caste or corporation, and the highest for reviling gods and sanctuaries." (A.3.18.12, 247) It is unclear how strictly this was enforced, because Kautilya apparently approved of actors making fun of almost anything. "[Actors] may, at will, entertain by making fun of the (customs of) countries, castes, families, schools and love-affairs." (A.4.1.61, 258) This approval of humor and entertainment is rare in the *Arthashastra*, which is almost always a somber and serious book. Above all, one must not criticize the king. "He shall cause the tongue to be rooted out of one who reviles the king or divulges secret counsel or spreads evil news (about the king)." (A.4.11.21, 285)

## Torture and Assassination

Kautilya also defended the practice of torturing a suspect who cannot prove his or her innocence. "In case of corroboration by persons proving his innocence, he shall be cleared of guilt; otherwise, he shall be put to torture." (A.4.8.4, 274) Kautilya contended that "one should put to torture one whose guilt is found to be probable," but not a pregnant woman or a Brahmin. (A.4.8.17-18, 27, 276-77) The ordinary fourfold torture consisted mostly of some kinds of beating, but for "grave offenders," Kautilya outlined the eighteen-fold torture that included "two scorpion-bindings" and other assorted painful procedures. (A.4.8.21-23, 276; see Agrawal 1990, 32-33) I cannot agree with Dikshitar who generously concludes that in Kautilya's *Arthashastra* there is "no mention of torture to elicit confession of a crime." (Dikshitar 1993, 166) Choudhary concludes correctly that "spies also applied judicial torture to arrive at the truth." (Choudhary 1971, 166)

In a strange turn toward humanitarianism, Kautilya declared that a prisoner should be tortured only "on alternate days and one [torture] only on one day." (A.4.8.25, 277) In another passage in the *Arthashastra*, Kautilya urged leniency toward "the head of a religious order, an ascetic, a sick person, one exhausted by hunger, thirst or a journey, a foreigner, one groaning under a fine, and an indigent person." (A.3.20.21, 252) He was well aware that a person, out of fear or desperation, might declare himself or herself guilty in the face of punishment or torture. (A.4.8.12, 275) To complicate all this further, Kautilya urged that the authorities clear out a prison at least every five days and either fine people or make them work or administer corporal punishment. (A.2.36.46, 189)

Torture was common in the ancient world. What surprises me is not that torture existed, but that Kautilya is just about the only political thinker to discuss it openly and defend its practice in somewhat carefully circumscribed circumstances.

Kautilya also repeatedly defended the practice of assassination; he labeled assassination as "silent punishment" or sometimes the "weeding of thorns" (although this might just involve arrest and punishment [A.2.4-5, 265-68]). This is not a topic buried toward the back of a five hundred page book, but rather discussed early in Book 1. "And he should pacify with money and honour those who are resentful with good reason, those resentful without reason, by silent punishment, also those who do what is inimical to the king." (A.1.11.21, 23) His defense is implicit here; to protect the king one must sometimes use violence against those who are dangerous. Defending the kingdom and the social order comprised of the four *varnas* was Kautilya's highest goal, and often this requires assassination. "But against those treasonable principal officers, who cause harm to the kingdom, (and) who, being favourites or being united, cannot be suppressed openly, [the king] should employ 'silent punishment,' finding pleasure in (doing his) duty." (A.5.1.4, 292) After listing for a number of paragraphs ways of assassinating people by poison and deceit, Kautilya remarked. "Thus [the king] should behave towards treasonable and unrighteous persons, not towards others. He should take from the kingdom fruits as they ripen, as from a garden; he should avoid unripe (fruit) that causes an uprising, for fear of his own destruction." (A.5.2.69-70, 301) Whereas Kautilya was clearly admonishing a king not to kill righteous people, he did not do so as much from a moral standpoint, but from a practical political one, that is, that a ruler perceived to be killing or imprisoning good citizens will inevitably face opposition to his rule. Similarly, in Book 14 Kautilya claimed that, "For the sake of protecting the four *varnas*, he should use secret practices against the unrighteous." (A.14.1.1, 494) Elsewhere, he urged that "secret practices" be used against "the treasonable." (A.5.6.48, 313) Secret practices turn out to be magical weapons—potions that cause leprosy or cholera or blindness, an iguana that can kill on sight—fantastic recipes that one wonders if Kautilya really believed were effective. "[The king] should cause fright to the enemy with (these) evil, miraculous portents[,] because it is for the consolidation of the kingdom." (A.14.2.45, 502; and A.14.1-2) With these secret practices, a king "should destroy the enemies and protect his own people." (A.14.3.88, 509) After one has conquered an enemy, one should use "silent punishment" against "those capable of injuring or those brooding over the master's destruction." (A.13.5.17, 492; see Agrawal 1990, 45-47)

## Was Kautilya Immoral?

Innocent people died if Chandragupta and Bindusara followed Kautilya's advice of weeding thorns and silent punishment, for in assassinating traitors, Kautilya was more than willing to use or to entrap the innocent. For example, after bribing a brother of a treasonable officer and having him kill the officer, Kautilya advocated that the king execute the innocent brother for fratricide. Or again, tell the son of a treasonable officer that he—the son—is actually the crown prince and will attain the throne if he kills his father. Once he has killed his father, execute the son for patricide. Or once more, put poison in one's own food served by a treasonable officer and his cook, and kill them both for attempted murder. (A.5.1.5-7, 15-18, 30-32, 292-94) Finally, to win a battle or to take a fort, he was quite willing to sacrifice his own loyal spies in the enemy's midst. (A.13.3.12, 481-82)

Kautilya even acknowledged that a king may have to sacrifice a wife or a son. "A king protects the kingdom (only) when (he is himself) protected from persons near him and from enemies, first from his wives and sons." (A.1.17.1, 39) Kautilya quoted with approval a predecessor's axiom that "princes, like crabs, are father-eaters." (Cited by Kosambi 1994, 144; see A.1.17.4-5, 39) Despite generally approving of the practice of passing the throne to the eldest son, Kautilya did not want that to be an inviolable rule, because he recognized that many eldest sons are "undisciplined" and hence unfit to rule. (A.1.17.51-52, 43) If a prince is disaffected, immoral, and "incorrigible," then a king should try to reeducate the prince and exile the prince, but if necessary, "secret agents should kill [the prince] with weapon or poison." (A.1.18.14, 45; and Book 1.17-18, passim.)

In the killing of innocents and in the killing of a prince, those who see Kautilya as nothing but immoral have some credible evidence. When Kosambi claims that in Kautilya's *Arthashastra*, "there is not the least pretence at morality," (Kosambi 1994, 142) he points out that not only did Kautilya advise a king to protect himself against a prince, but Kautilya could also not resist explaining to a prince in disfavor how to overthrow his father. (Kosambi 1994, 145; A.1.18.5-12, 43-44) By advising a king to kill a threatening prince, has Kautilya not demonstrated to bad kings how they might not perpetuate their evil? What if the prince is good and the king is evil? And by maintaining that saving the country or preserving the social order or rescuing a people from anarchy sometimes requires what we ordinarily regard as "evil" means, such as killing some who are innocent, hasn't Kautilya sanctioned killing or cruelty or injustice for any king who claims to be working for and upholding the general good? Kautilya usually referred to killing the unrighteous or treasonable, but in one passage he urged that women should be used "against the wicked, for spying, killing or making them blunder." (A.2.27.30, 162) Doesn't advocating spying upon and killing "the wicked" give enormous latitude or moral and political justification to a ruler to do just about whatever he or she wishes, no matter how violent and cruel? Is Ghoshal right when he says that we find Kautilya "frequently inculcating rules of a grossly unscrupulous nature on the plea of public interest and without the least pretence of moral disapproval"? (Ghoshal 1923, 148) Was the ancient poet Bāna (seventh century C.E.) fair in describing Kautilya's *Arthashastra* as "merciless in precepts and rich in cruelty"? (Majumdar 1960, 65)

How would Kautilya respond to this charge of immorality? First, he would note, as we saw previously and as one can see repeatedly in his *Arthashastra* that morality is usually the best policy, that social justice brings practical political results. Over and over Kautilya repeated that a greedy and cruel king, one whose desires are spinning out of control, will face rebellion and loss of power. Similarly, he warned of attacking a righteous and just kingdom, because that king's subjects would fight like tigers to defend a good king. How much easier it is to conquer the wicked! Second, he would say that the political world is a morally complicated morass, a dirty place, in which sometimes one must undertake what we would ordinarily call "evil" actions to bring good results. Kautilya would say that he did not cause this problem, and he did not make the political world so complicated, but rather he is just telling his readers about the reality of politics. And in this political world, a ruler who avoids any action that we traditionally call "evil" will bring ruin to himself or herself, as well as to the citizens of the realm. After discussing the necessities of occasional assassination, Kautilya concluded, "In this way, the kingdom continues in the succession of his sons and grand-sons, free from danger caused by men. He should employ 'silent punish-ment' towards his own party or that of the enemy, without hesitation, being possessed of forbearance in respect of the future and the present." (A.5.1.56-57, 296)

The argument here is that we judge political actions by results, not intentions, and that sometimes—by no means always—the ends do justify the means. This is the agonizing reality for the political actor. *If* sacrificing an innocent person is absolutely necessary to bring a long period of prosperity, both material and spiritual, then it would be "immoral" to abstain from that violent action. We cannot always apply private morality to political matters, or, as K. M. Agrawal remarks, Kautilya was the first thinker "to make a distinction between ethics and political science." (Agrawal 1990, xv) As Drekmeier observes, Kautilya argued that "moral principles must be subordinated to the interests of the state inasmuch as the moral order depends upon the continued existence of the state." (Drekmeier 1962, 201)

Machiavelli made Kautilya's argument some eighteen centuries after Kautilya. As he wrote in *The Prince*, "for how we live is so far removed from how we ought to live, that he who abandons what is done for what ought to be done, will rather learn to bring about his own ruin. . . . Therefore it is necessary for a prince, who wishes to maintain himself, to learn how not to be good, and to use this knowledge and not to use it, according to the necessity of the case." (Machiavelli, Ch.15) Machiavelli assumed, I think, that the reader would understand that the "ruin" in question is the ruin of the prince and all of his subjects. Moreover, he did not say that a prince ought always to act in traditionally evil or bad ways, but only "according to the necessity of the case." This means that one who rules will make mistakes, because we cannot predict a human future the way we can calculate the motions of planets. Even the noblest political actor will sorrowfully find that some violent actions bring great good, and sometimes they turn out to have been tragically unnecessary. As Max Weber stated, politics is not a place to save one's soul, but it is the only place one may save one's nation. Machiavelli wanted us to understand this tenet of political realism so much that he put this proposition even more bluntly later in *The Prince*. A prince "cannot observe all those things which are considered good in men, being obliged, in order to maintain the state, to act against faith, against charity, against humanity, and against religion." (Machiavelli, Ch. 18) To those who think that always acting in a decent, humane, and kind way will bring "good" results, Weber said, "it is *not* true that good can follow only from good and evil only from evil, but that often the opposite is true. Anyone who fails to see this is, indeed, a political infant." (Cited in Boesche 1996, 121)

In the Jain version of the legend of Chandragupta and Kautilya—and this is only unsubstantiated legend—we find a third warrior named Parvataka who joined these two to defeat the Nanda kings. After the three had conquered the Nanda kings and were deciding how to found a kingdom and consolidate political power, Kautilya conspired with Chandragupta to deny Parvataka needed medical care and consequently let him die. (Bhargava 1996, 121-26) What is striking about this story is that it is so similar to legends about the founding of other civilizations, similar to Romulus killing his brother Remus and founding Rome and similar to Cain killing Abel and going off to establish cities and civilization. Is it possible that these stories are suggesting that in doing something great, something such as founding a nation, a great crime is always committed, that sometimes in this imperfect world great good emerges from great evil?

Kautilya frequently defended justice and compassion. On page 8 of his book, he said that we all have the following duties: "abstaining from injury (to living creatures), truthfulness, uprightness, freedom from malice, compassionateness and forbearance." (A.1.3.13, 8) It is just that compassion is sometimes a luxury that a king, and a kingdom, cannot afford. Some Indian scholars want to wipe away Kautilya's discussions of spies, arrest on suspicion, torture, and assassination. Ritu Kohli, for example, wants to correct the misconception that Kautilya "was a cruel, manipulative, tyrant and a believer in the policy of expediency." (Kohli 1995, xi) Radhagobinda Basak embraces, without the least hesitation or reservation, "the wonderful system of espionage." (Basak 1967, 4) B. Bhagat hails Kautilya as a "patriot" who loved "non-violence." (Bhagat 1990, 189-90) This sort of unreserved apologetic is not really an argument but rather an uncritical eulogy that impoverishes Kautilya and removes the richness, the depth, and the intricacies of his arguments.

## The Primacy of the State

Kautilya is given much credit for offering one of the first comprehensive theories of the state by discussing the seven constituent elements of the state—"the king, the minister, the country, the fortified city, the treasury, the army and the ally." (A.6.1.1, 314; see Sharma 1991, 38; Roy 1992, 98; Mishra 1965, 27) We don't know that this notion is original with Kautilya; we find the elements of the state in almost exactly this order in the *Laws of Manu*, a book with ancient roots but not written down until well after Kautilya. (*Laws of Manu,* 229) For the purposes of this book, it is most important to note that Kautilya relied upon a centralized state—indeed, advocated an extraordinarily powerful state—like no thinker in India or elsewhere had before. The king and the state should dominate both Brahmins and powerful economic classes.

Whereas Kautilya was careful to show respect to Brahmin priests and defend their status, he clearly saw religion as subordinate to the interests of the state. Of course, in almost all cultures, there is frequently tension between secular and priestly power. In the *Rig Veda*, we see that Brahmin priests crowned kings. "I have brought you here; remain among us. . . . Stand stead-fast here, like Indra; and here uphold the kingdom." (*Rig Veda*,

64) Interestingly, all mention of priests crowning kings is absent in Kautilya's *Arthashastra.* (Saletore 1963, 302) In addition, "the Brahmin must walk before the king," and the king depended on Brahmins "for the correct formulations of the sacrifices and the correct propitiation of innumerable deities and noxious forces." (Derrett 1976, 600, 603) Moreover, Kautilya's proposed kingdom was much less advantageous in its laws to Brahmins than were more traditional forms of rule. (Saletore 1963, 73) As Ghoshal puts it, Kautilya made one of the earliest and most dramatic contributions to political thought by "emancipating politics from the tutelage of theology and raising it to the dignity of an independent science." (Ghoshal 1923, 114-15) By focusing on the political world as it is and trying to master that world, Kautilya did not "treat political problems in terms of either ethical standards or religious dogmas." (Saletore 1963, 53) Throughout his *Arthashastra,* in matters of importance Kautilya repeatedly made certain that "priestly power [was] made subordinate to royal power." (Sharma 1991, 263) For example, in key passages, he stated that, when in conflict, citizens must hold the king's edict to be superior to any other agreements, laws, or customs; no one should have a divided allegiance, and as a consequence, a royal edict must have more authority than religious practices. (A.3.1.38-45, 194-96; Sharma 1991, 263)

There is more evidence in the *Arthashastra* that Kautilya wanted religion to be secondary to state power. For example, Kautilya's state should take responsibility for building most shrines and temples, (A.2.4.17-20, 70) which would certainly make religious authorities dependent on the state. Moreover, there is some evidence that the state controlled much of the wealth and property of the temples and shrines. (Sharma 1991, 264) Probably most important is what Kautilya omitted. When he listed in a well-known passage the seven constituent elements of the state—"the king, the minister, the country, the fortified city, the treasury, the army, and the ally" (A.6.1.1, 314)—he omitted entirely any mention of religion or the power of Brahmin priests. (Sharma 1991, 40) By contrast, when Megasthenes reported on the seven castes or classes that he found in India, he put the philosophers or Brahmin priests first! (McCrindle 1960, 38) Before the Mauryan kings, India's monarchies had been akin to theocracies, (Singh 1993, 46) but no longer. Reading the *Arthashastra* closely, one occasionally can stumble over hints that sometimes Kautilya regarded religion as an obstacle to royal power that must be overcome. For instance, in a passage about war, Kautilya wrote, "Hindrances to gain are: passion, anger, nervousness, pity, shyness, ignobleness, haughtiness, a sympathetic nature, *regard for the other world, piousness.*" (A.9.4.25, 419, my emphasis) Kautilya did not want religious power, religious practice, or religious concern to compete with the state for power and authority, and because he wanted to conquer and expand the state, he did not want a religious ethic to interfere with military greatness. Says Drekmeier, "[Kautilya] must be understood as attempting to liberate the heroic ideal from the debilitating influences of religion." (Drekmeier 1962, 157)

Put bluntly, Kautilya liked religion when he could make it useful to the state. (For a contrary view, see Bhagat 1990, 190.) For example, Kautilya stated that brave men who die in battle, "reach in one moment even beyond those (worlds), which, Brahmins, desirous of heaven, reach by a large number of sacrifices." (A.10.3.30, 440) Similarly, "bards and panegyrists should describe the attainment of heaven by the brave and the absence of heaven for cowards." (A.10.3.43, 441) In the enemy camp, "soothsayers, interpreters of omens, astrologers, reciters of *Purāṇas*, seers, and secret agents" should frighten the enemy by declaring that Kautilya's king has been "meeting with divinities." (A.13.1.7-8, 475) In all of these examples, religion is useful, but mentioned on a par with astrologers who announce the king's omniscience, declare the king's "association with divine agencies," and "fill the enemy's side with terror." (A.10.3.33, 440) The king must also "make (Brahmins) recite blessings invoking victory and securing heaven." (A.10.3.34, 440) In natural calamities such as fire, floods, and famine, Kautilya urged people to pray to gods and to turn to holy ascetics and magicians, to attempt any measure that might be useful, to put trust in anyone who might share the blame in a disaster! (A.4.3.12,44, 263, 265) After Kautilya listed disasters that can befall the state such as fire, floods, disease, famine and so forth, he said that, "overcoming them is through prostration before gods and Brahmins." If there is too much rain or drought or "demoniac creation," then the state can overcome these disasters with "rites prescribed in the Artharvaveda and undertaken by holy men." (A.9.7.82-84, 432) If Kautilya had his way, whom do you the think the people would blame for such natural disasters?

Priests and astrologers—in fact, all purveyors of superstition (Sharma 1954, 223-25)—are simply there to reinforce and to serve state power, and Kautilya unquestionably wanted royal power to command priestly power. As Radhakrishna Choudhary puts it so well, "Religion was made even a means for accomplishing political ends." (Choudhary 1971, 244) As Banerji notes, Kautilya was willing to use almost any kind of deception to fool and control all subjects. (Banerji 1993, 302, 187) Sharma says correctly that "a distinctive feature of the *Arthashastra* politics as expounded by Kautilya is the deliberate use of superstition by the ruling class to hoodwink and overawe the masses." (Sharma 1991, 271) Sharma is correct about the use of superstition, but I think he is wrong in his assertion about ruling classes, because Kautilya also wanted the state to control the leading classes.

Obviously classes existed in ancient India, and in general Brahmins and Kshatriyas formed a ruling class, although certainly tensions understandably existed between the two. Sibesh Bhattacharya, in an excellent article, outlines the tensions between Brahmins and Kshatriyas—"It is interesting that while one strand of the theory of kingship represented in the sacerdotal literature asserts the begetting of kingship by the priests through the agency of sacrifice, another strand points to the divine origin of kingship"—and concludes that these classes formed a ruling elite, but he never gave evidence that this was true in fact, not just in theory, for the Mauryan empire. (Bhattacharya 1984, 14, 19, 1 respectively) The question at hand is what influence these powerful classes would have had on the state that Kautilya described, and I argue that if Kautilya had his way—and we probably will never know enough about Chandragupta Maurya's rule to know if he did—the state would retain considerable independence from, and make use of, these key classes. This may not be so unusual as it sounds; Weber, and even Marx, saw that at certain moments in history a strong state can have interests of its own and considerable autonomy from powerful classes. (Boesche 1996, 262-71, 367-70) Even Sharma, who talks about the "class character" of the Mauryan state, used Engels for his analysis, and spoke of "the ruling classes," (Sharma 1991, 39-40) admits that, "Kautilya's legislation introduces a liberal interlude, its object being to provide a scheme of imperial laws overriding petty considerations of caste. . . . Kautilya tries to lessen the rigours of class legislation." (Sharma 1991, 246) Kosambi argues this position well. Every state, he acknowledges, is "class-based," but Kautilya's state appears "fantastic" to us, because the state—as we shall see in the next chapter—was the chief landowner and in control of most industries and most production. As Kosambi concludes, "The ruling class was, if not created by and for the state, at least greatly augmented as part of the administration." (Kosambi 1994, 143) Satya Deva may well be right in arguing that the bureaucracy under Chandragupta might have "[functioned] as a ruling class." (Deva 1984, 812) However, I believe that the state with the king in control—and not a dominant economic class—was primary. (Kangle 1992, 139)

Is there evidence supporting this proposition in the *Arthashastra*? First, we find that Kautilya disliked traders who were not supervised and therefore not controlled by the state. To go from the world of the *Rāmāyana* to Kautilya's world is to travel from a feudal economy to an urban economy of trade and finance, (Nagarajan 2 1992, 266-68) and we find that Kautilya disliked these new classes. As A. Ghosh points out, the rise of cities includes the rise of merchants, (Ghosh 1973, 22) and it is almost as if Kautilya had an easier time appeasing Brahmins and Kshatriyas than he did traders who were Vaishyas. Kautilya scoffed bitterly that,"Traders, joining and raising and lowering the (prices of) goods, make a profit of one hundred *panas* on one *pana*." (A.8.4.36, 399)[2] Kautilya regarded traders as "thieves." In response to this belief, "Not only did the State associate itself closely with the trading and industrial classes, but it also undertook manufactures and trading on its own account." (Ghoshal 1996, 276, 275) Second, strongly urging that large estates be broken up in the process of inheritance, Kautilya came very close to outlawing primogeniture or the practice of leaving the entire estate to the oldest son. If Kautilya's policies toward inheritance had been followed, over time there would be no large landowners—no concentration of economic power—to oppose the state. Said Kautilya, "in the case of partition during his life-time, the father shall not show special favor to any one. And he shall not, without ground, exclude any one from inheritance. . . . There is to be an equal division of debts and property." (A.3.5.16-17, 22, 210) Jefferson was proud of having done this in Virginia! Finally, Kautilya wanted the king to find his basis for support in ordinary people who were not in the two upper classes. For instance, he supported unions and guilds. (A.3.14.12-18, 240) In another passage, in favoring a sick king over a new king, Kautilya preferred a sick king "who is rooted among the subjects," (A.8.2.18, 392) rather than a new king with no popular ties. And Kautilya also looked, as we will see later, to a popular army relying on Kshatriyas, Vaishyas, and Shūdras; indeed he thought Brahmins were poor soldiers who quit fighting too quickly. As Drekmeier has rightly observed, Kautilya was "a champion of the Shūdras," (Drekmeier 1962, 198) who regarded them as "freeborn citizens," most of whom had Aryan status and all of whom could be called upon to serve in the army. Far from seeking to ally his king and state with some wealthy ruling classes, Kautilya endeavored to have the king and the state control all classes, make use of all classes, and maintain widespread popular support. Maybe this was a mistake. V. Subramaniam raises a fascinating question. Did the Mauryan empire collapse more quickly than the other empires in the ancient world because the state demanded that the king, ruling through officials in state institutions, do too much by himself, rather than allying himself with one or more powerful classes. "Kautilya staked too much on a powerful state—with powers to disrobe monks, tax the rich merchants into abject submission, and even keep the Brahmins in their place." (Subramaniam 1998, 99)

The popular support that Kautilya envisioned did not include active citizenship. In the Vedic period, kings had to manipulate or to cooperate with

Central Assemblies, or *samitis*; but these had disappeared by 500 B.C.E. (Altekar 1962, 66, 139-45) Whereas there was no genuine ideal of citizenship in the Mauryan empire, (Drekmeier 1962, 147) there was a warrior ideal, and Kautilya wanted to keep it that way. Kautilya knew that the best way to depoliticize subjects is to keep them isolated in private space and in their private lives, so that they cannot meet, discuss, and organize, and throughout the *Arthashastra*, Kautilya frequently recommended ways to keep people apart and close off public space where they might gather. For example, in proposing a curfew from 9:00 p.m. to 3:30 a.m., Kautilya sought penalties for anyone out at night, and this certainly fastened people to their private homes and prohibited them from gathering in public. (Mookerji 1988, 135) Kautilya knew that fear isolates. Similarly, Kautilya wanted people to leave public business to the state, stay in their private homes, and not even get together with their neighbors. "House-owners should live near the front doors of their own houses, not collecting together at night." (A.2.36.21, 186) Even in the palace, Kautilya wanted each to be isolated. "And every one (in the palace) should live in his own quarters and should not move to the quarters of another." (A.1.20.22, 51)

As we have already seen, Aśoka prohibited public meetings, and it may have been an idea that he got from Kautilya, but certainly outlawing public meetings controlled the populace. As Thapar notes, "The suppression of these popular meetings and assemblies is in conformity with the idea of strict centralization. Such gatherings may have been feared as occasions for attacks on the king's new ideas." (Thapar 1997, 152) Demanding that subjects work hard in their specialized functions of the division of labor also leaves no time for public life. "For, men being of a nature similar to that of horses," wrote Kautilya, "change when employed in works. . . . They should carry out the works according to orders, without concerting together." (A.2.9.3, 5, 89) In discussing the settlement of new lands, Kautilya prohibited amusements that would bring people together and reduce the time for work. "And there should be no parks there nor halls for recreation. Actors, dancers, singers, musicians, professional story-tellers or minstrels shall not create obstruction in the work (of the people)." (A.2.1.33-34, 58; see Nagarajan 2 1992, 74) (In fact, music, dance, drama, satires against the powerful, horse-racing, jesters, wrestlers, boxers, acrobats, jugglers, snake charmers, and magicians all entertained at festivals in ancient India, but many like Kautilya frowned upon such entertainment. Dancers, for example, lost their caste status. [Das 1994, 156, 189-94; Banerji 1993, 160-71]) Kosambi remarks rightly that banning meetings and forcing people to work long and hard at their jobs means that, "the idiocy of village life was deliberately fostered by early state policy." (Kosambi 1994, 150-51)

The only exception that I can find to this banning of public meetings is in Kautilya's apparent approval of guilds, although we know very little about their actual operation. Shyamsunder Nigam suggests that, "guilds operated on a democratic basis. . . . They were the connecting links between the state and the public," (Nigam 1975, 55) but I am not satisfied with the evidence offered. Bandyopadhyaya argues more convincingly that the government controlled the guilds, because, "The powerful Kautilya government could not brook such independence on the part of these combinations of artisans or workmen." (Bandyopadhyaya 1927, 201) Kautilya wanted unions to divide pay among workers "as agreed upon or in equal proportions," he saw unions as disciplining workers, and he apparently wanted workers rotated off a job after seven days, (A.3.14.18, 12-17, 240; A.2.4.16, 69) perhaps as Kangle says, "to prevent direct and close relations being established between individual workmen and the employer." (Kangle 1992, 240) We do know from history that there were guilds for merchants, weavers, washermen, goldsmiths, doctors, musicians, and occasionally Brahmin priests. (Saletore 1975, 527-28) Kautilya did not make a distinction between guilds and unions, and it is possible that he saw them not as tools for organizing, but as state-controlled organizations for disciplining workers. Certainly, like every other institution, guilds were subject to state regulation. (Sen 1967, 175, 179-80)

Kautilya knew that one can more easily conquer a disunited and isolated populace, and that means that the state can more easily dominate and control such a depoliticized mass of subjects. "And subjects, contending among themselves, benefit (the king) by their mutual rivalry." (A.8.4.19, 398) Lands with "people disunited" (A.7.11.18-19, 356; Chousalkar 1990, 38) are more easily conquered. Because there are no spontaneous revolts, and because organized opposition requires leaders, Kautilya thought that if the king killed the leaders, then the people would fall back into an unorganized and dispersed isolation. "Disaffection can be overcome by the suppression of the leaders." (A.7.5.35, 336; Chousalkar 1990, 38-42) If secret agents can "sow discord" among an enemy and foment "mutual hatred, enmity or strife," if these agents can "start quarrels" within the enemy camp, then Kautilya's army could more easily conquer. (A.11.1.6-8, 455) In the end, he would settle families of a conquered people on available land, and "fix a penalty if they come together." (A.11.1.17-19, 455-56) The domestic corollary to this advice on conquering a disunited enemy is obvious; keep subjects apart, alone, in private space, and powerless to organize, and the king and the state can control the populace quite easily.

## An Administered People

If Kautilya's science of politics was put into practice by the Mauryan governments, then the king's extraordinarily far-reaching bureaucracy controlled his subjects as much as any people in the ancient world. (Basak 1967, 1-16) U. Ghoshal comments that Kautilya's detailed analysis of the bureaucratic administration of the state took him well beyond Machiavelli's discussion of how a state works. (Ghoshal 1923, 155) While we cannot know if the empires of Chandragupta, Bindusara, and Aśoka actually had such an extensive system of administration, Kautilya described a detailed bureaucracy unlike anything in other ancient empires such as those in Egypt, Persia, or China. If the bureaucracy in reality even approached what Kautilya suggested in theory, one reason must have been that some castes had government service as one possible occupation. "Generally speaking, the higher administrative positions seem to have been monopolised by [Brahmins] and [Kshatriyas]." (Das 1994, 145)

We will explore the economy in more depth later, but Kautilya wanted the state to control much of the economy. For example, "The Director of Stores should cause to be built a treasury, a warehouse, a store for forest produce, an armoury, and a prison-house." (A.2.5.1, 72) And, "The Superintendent of the Armoury should cause to be made machines for use in battles, for the defence of forts and for assault on the enemies' cities, also weapons." (A.2.18.1, 131) The Director of Forest Produce should establish factories for making all kinds of things of wood "for ensuring livelihood and protection of the city." (A.2.17.17, 131) The Director of Trade should set prices for most commodities "so as to favour the subjects" and not allow profits "injurious" to ordinary people. (A.2.16.5-6, 127) Kautilya's government should even have a Superintendent of Courtesans who would hire courtesans, place them in government houses, tax and presumably license them, and be responsible for hiring teaches who will teach courtesans "knowledge of the arts of singing, playing on musical instruments, reciting, dancing, acting, writing, painting, playing on the lute, the flute and the drum, reading the thoughts of others, preparing perfumes and garlands, entertaining in conversation, shampooing and the courtesan's art [presumably sexual pleasure]." (A.2.27.28, 161)

Has there ever been such a centralized bureaucratic administration that sought to control such details of ordinary people's lives? The wisdom and command of the king were to be everywhere, manifested in every government official, but the king himself was not present. The king "should conceal, as a tortoise does his limbs, any (limb) of his own that may have become exposed." (A.1.15.60, 36) While the power of the king was everywhere simultaneously, he himself was above the administration of everyday life. The king exercised this power through an extraordinarily extensive professional bureaucracy, probably from subcastes or *jātis* in which one was born for government service, from which the king chose officials based on merit, not a system of spoils. (Mehta and Thakkar 1980, 102)

If detailed record-keeping is a sign of a new despotism, as some such as Weber and Foucault have claimed, then indeed Kautilya's kingdom was despotic. Kautilya wanted an extraordinarily detailed census with officials visiting every village to see how much an individual village should pay in taxes, how many men it should supply to the army, and so forth. A revenue officer should look after five to ten villages, recording how many people live in each, how many in each *varna*, how many in each occupation, the ages of each person, how many and what kind of animals, and so on. (A.2.35.1-5, 182-83) Not only was there a detailed census of the people, but Kautilya declared, "They should maintain a record in writing of (every) elephant"! (A.2.211, 60) A centralized Records Office should be built "facing the east or the north" (A.2.7.1, 80) (No southern exposure to the sun?), and it should have detailed records of the income of all departments, whether the income of each department had increased or decreased, the materials used, and other various detailed records of wages, expenses, and revenue. Of course the Superintendent of the Records office should have "the activity (of departments) watched by spies," (A.2.7.9, 82) and should keep detailed accounts of all income and expenditures. "After hearing the totals of income, expenditure, and balance, he should cause the balance to be taken away (to the treasury)." (A.2.7.18, 83) A Superintendent of Passports must issue sealed passes before one could "enter or leave the countryside," (A.2.34.2, 181) a practice that might constitute the first passbooks and passports in world history. All traders coming into the country must have an "identity-pass," and customs officials should record in writing what each caravan brought into the country. (A.2.21.2, 142) If, as Weber said, written records and double entry bookkeeping are signs of a modern, emerging capitalist economy, then how do we make sense of Kautilya's centrally planned economy? And if Foucault saw a new form of domination in the state sorting and categorizing us while we all watch and superintend one another, what do we call Kautilya's proposed state? One reason that Kautilya fascinates the modern reader is that he defies all the usual categories we have of the ancient world.

Kautilya spoke of a "science of building," (A.2.3.3, 61-62) and he gave detailed instructions about how to lay out a city, including how wide the various roads should be and how far apart the buildings should be. Seeking a rationally planned city, Kautilya wanted "dealers in perfume, flowers and liquids, makers of articles of toilet and Kshatriyas [to] live in the eastern quarter," while "workers in metals and jewels and Brahmins should live in the northern quarter." (A.2.4.9, 15, 68-69) Having established his city, Kautilya sought to control it. Each city should have a City Superintendent who would appoint section officers. "The section officer (should look after) a group of ten families or twenty or forty families. He should find out the number of individuals, men and women, in that (group), according to caste, family-name and occupation, also their income and expenditure." (A.2.36.2-3, 185) The only modern example that I can think of that sought to watch over each citizen to this extent is modern China under Mao. In the case of town planning, Kautilya's proposals were probably more theoretical than actually workable. As William Kirk says, "In view of the noisome Indian cities of medieval and later times it is difficult to imagine the orderly, disciplined cities depicted in the *Arthashastra*." (Kirk 1978, 74)

Kautilya seemed to have an obsession with making everything in the kingdom just right. The Superintendent of Horses "should cause a bath to be given horses twice a day," (A.2.30.50, 174) the Superintendent of Elephants must build stables and stalls for elephants to exact specifications, (A.2.31.2-4, 175) the City Superintendent must fine individuals one-eighth of a *pana* "for throwing dirt on the road" and double that fine for "blocking it with muddy water," (A.2.36.26, 186) judges should make certain that each house has a window "high up" which individuals must cover when they are at home, (A.3.8.16-17, 217) judges should also make certain that, except for Brahmins, "One who does not contribute his share [of work] in a stage-show shall not witness it," (A.3.10.37, 225) and judges should fine individuals a specified amount for harming "bushes and creepers bearing flowers or fruit or yielding shade." (A.3.19.29, 250) Nor did Kautilya hesitate in his attempts to legislate or mandate morality. For example, "for those who do not go to the rescue [of one drowning in a flood], the fine is twelve *panas*, except in the case of those without canoes." (A.4.3.9, 263) And, one must be fined if he or she vilifies another for "leprosy, madness, impotence and so on." (A.3.18.4, 246) Moreover, a husband who does not have sex with his wife at the correct time of month was fined 96 *panas*, so even sexual activity was supposed to be the concern of the state. (Thomas 1964, 73) As T. N. Ramaswamy put it, in Kautilya's *Arthashastra*, "everyday life in all its multifarious aspects comes in for careful regulation and adjustment, from the cooking-pot to the crown." (Ramaswamy 1994, 32)

It is worth reiterating that it is unclear how much of this detailed control the Mauryan kings actually achieved. Could the centralized administration of a country in the ancient world really control life at the village level? Thapar says that under the Mauryan state "local regions were left relatively untampered as long as they provided the required revenue." (Thapar 1992, 156) However, in her book on Aśoka, Thapar also claims that under Mauryan administration, "the king had control over even the most remote part of the empire. An efficient bureaucracy was essential to this." (Thapar 1997, 123) Even Kautilya mentioned cases, such as deciding boundaries or property lines, in which local government, and not the central government appointees should make decisions. (A.3.9.10, 219) I seriously doubt that the centralized state reached into village life as much as Kautilya wanted. As R. Choudhary says, in ancient India, "Rural politics was, to a great extent, independent of state politics." (Choudhary 1971, 195)

## Notes

1. For the classifications of spies in Kautilya's time, see Banerji 1993, 297-98.

2. In South India, when the cities dwindled and the trading economy disappeared, the merchants were replaced by feudal landowners who submitted to temple worship and ruled along with the Brahmins. (Kennedy 1976, 14-15)

# Chapter 4

# THE ECONOMY: A SOCIALIST MONARCHY

The most important element of the state, according to Kautilya, is neither the government nor the army, but the treasury. "Spiritual good and sensual pleasures," he wrote, "depend on material well-being." (A.1.7.7, 14) In a sense the good life of the kingdom, the well-being, or *yogakshema,* of the people will never occur if the economy is in shambles. This is one point that Kautilya's readers cannot miss. "All undertakings are dependent first on the treasury." (A.2.8.1, 85) Every good in political life—peace, conquest, order, the correct social and class structure, *dharma*, and so on—depends on the state acquiring wealth and using it wisely. "Men, without wealth, do not attain their objects even with hundreds of efforts; objects are secured through objects, as elephants are through elephants set to catch them." (A.9.4.27, 419) After declaring early in Book 1 that "material well-being alone is supreme," (A.1.7.6, 14), Kautilya continued later by saying that the king will be happy only when his subjects are happy, and, "Therefore, being ever active, the king should carry out the management of material well-being." (A.1.19.35, 34, 47) In this statement we find the key to understanding the importance of the economy for Kautilya. The king can rule properly—defend the country, uphold the four *varnas*, govern like a concerned father, make sure that individuals are not exploited by greed, and bring about Kautilya's vision of social justice—only if there is material prosperity. Thus, Kautilya was not defending endless wealth or economic "development"—he had no notion of that—but he was saying the calamity of poverty would defeat anything a good king needs and wants to do. "And the treasury, ensuring (the success of) all endeavors, is the means of deeds of piety and sensual pleasure." (A.8.1.49, 388) The goals are always "well-being and security" (A.8.1.23, 387) from enemies from both within and without.

Whereas many thinkers in both the European and Asian traditions might declare that religion is most important, or that the political constitution is central to achieving peace and justice, or whereas some such as Machiavelli might see a disciplined army as central to political well-being, Kautilya singled out the treasury. Without a treasury, there is no effective army. Whereas Machiavelli warned against relying on wealth and hiring mercenaries and instead recommended a popular army with republican virtues, Kautilya and Chandragupta Maurya had in fact used wealth to raise an army that successfully overthrew the Nanda kings. (Raychaudhuri 1996b, 144-45) No wonder Kautilya stressed the importance of wealth. "From the treasury the army comes into being. With the treasury and the army, the earth is obtained with the treasury as its ornament." (A.2.122.37, 110) Kautilya was not thinking of a mercenary army, and indeed I will show later that he favored a citizen army, but money allows one to pay and to equip soldiers. "With money, troops. . . are obtained." (A.7.9.30, 350) Indeed, "bravery, firmness, cleverness and large numbers are (found) among the country people." (A.8.1.30, 387) And even though he wanted a citizen army, he was not counting upon republican or patriotic fervor to ensure the loyalty of his soldiers. "The army, indeed, is rooted in the treasury. In the absence of the treasury, the army goes over to the enemy or kills the king." (A.8.1.48-49, 388) Kautilya said something that Machiavelli would never agree with, that is, that a king with money can conquer an enemy "by hiring or purchasing heroic men." (A.9.1.7, 406)

Because the treasury enables a king to pay soldiers and make military equipment, the army needs the treasury and the treasury must be protected by the army, so they will always be interrelated, but the treasury is ultimately more important. "For, the army is the means of acquiring and protecting the treasury, [but] the treasury that of the treasury and the army. Because it brings into being all objects, the calamity of the treasury is more serious." (A.8.1.51-52, 388-89) Most of all, Kautilya saw the treasury as a means of equipping well-trained soldiers—and providing elephants was central to Kautilya—who could then conquer anyone. "And his army, richly endowed with abundant might, horses, elephants, chariots and equipment, moves unhindered everywhere. And winning over and purchasing men of energy, those possessed of might, even women, children, lame and blind persons, have conquered the world." (A.9.1.9, 406) In addition, a treasury allows a king to build a fort, which in turn protects both the treasury and the kingdom. "In the absence of a fort, the treasury will fall into the hands of enemies. For it is seen that those with forts are not exterminated." (A.8.1.39-40, 388) Although Kautilya may have over-emphasized the importance of wealth to a citizen army, he persuasively demonstrated that Machiavelli understated the value of a healthy treasury.

Symbolically and practically, Kautilya wanted the king to use the "science of building" to build a fort for the treasury "in the centre of the country." (A.2.3.3, 61) Around the treasury fort should be three moats, a rampart, a parapet, turrets, and so on. "Outside (the fort), he should cause a covered road to be made that is strewn with knee-breakers, a mass of pikes, pits, concealed traps, barbed wires, 'serpent backs,' 'palm-leaves,' 'three peaks,' 'dog's jaws,' bars, 'jumping sandals,' frying pans and ponds." (A.2.3.15, 64; A.2.3, passim) Any thief who breaks into the treasury should suffer, not just the death penalty but a painful and prolonged death, or "death by torture." (A.2.5.20, 75)

## A Centralized Economy

No commentator has a phrase that adequately describes the economy that Kautilya outlined, because there has been nothing like it before or since the Mauryan empire. Wolpert declares the Mauryan economy was a "socialized monarchy," (Wolpert 1982, 60) and Basham calls it "a sort of state socialism" that "always left scope for the individual producer." (Basham 1963, 218) Others claim Kautilya established the first welfare state. Says Kohli, "Kautilya touched almost all of the aspects of human life, civilisation and culture with his concept of *Yogakshema* (welfare state, in the modern sense). Unfortunately, Kautilya's ideas on [a] welfare state did not receive the attention of foreign scholars, and it is generally believed that the idea of [a] welfare state is a modern one and originated in the West." (Kohli 1995, xi; see Altekar 1962, 332-33) Louis Dumont sees Kautilya's king running a benevolent feudal manor, perhaps a description that leads to the best understanding of Kautilya's economy. "Rather than speaking of monopolies," says Dumont, "or distinguishing a public sector in the economy, one should think of a manor." (Dumont 1962, 71) In fact all labels fail; it is best to describe Kautilya's economy in detail. It is worth noting how proud of Kautilya are so many Indian scholars; R. N. Saletore, for example, proclaims Kautilya "one of the greatest financial experts of all time." (Saletore 1975, 73)

Megasthenes, the Greek ambassador to Chandragupta's court, said that all land was owned by the king. Borrowing from Megasthenes, Diodorus wrote of those who worked the land; farmers or husbandmen "pay a land tribute to the king, because all India is property of the crown, and no private person is permitted to own land." (McCrindle 1960, 39; see Saletore 1975, 466) Using Megasthenes again, Diodorus went further to say that agricultural laborers lived their lives indifferent to the political and military turmoil that would determine the names of their masters. "But, further, there are usages observed by the Indians which contribute to prevent the occurrence of famine among them; for whereas among other nations it is usual in the context of war to ravage soil, and thus reduce it to an uncultivated waste, among the Indians, on the contrary, by whom husbandmen are regarded as a class that is sacred and inviolable, the tillers of the soil, even when battle is raging in their neighborhood, are undisturbed by any sense of danger, for the combatants on either side in waging the conflict make carnage of each other, but allow those engaged in husbandry to remain quite unmolested." (McCrindle 1960, 31-32) As for the class structure on the land, the mass of Shūdras were agricultural laborers who were working for those of higher *varnas* who owned land or leased land from the state. (Sharma 1990, 102, 161-63) Farming under the Mauryas must have been efficient, because Diodorus tells us that Megasthenes remarked that "famine has never visited India," (McCrindle 1960, 31) and even though modern historians know that statement is an exaggeration, Megasthenes must have been impressed by agricultural abundance. Megasthenes also reported seeing a strong, larger than ordinary, and well-nourished people in India. (McCrindle 1960, 30)

Modern scholars have struggled and disagreed over the question of whether Megasthenes was wrong in contending that the king owned all of the land. Kautilya himself sometimes gave the impression that the crown owned all land. In Book 2, Kautilya wrote, "He [meaning either the king or the Director of Agriculture] should allot to tax-payers arable fields for life. Unarable fields should not be taken away from those who are making them arable. He should take away (fields) from those who do not till them and give them to others." (A.2.1.8-10, 56) In short, untilled land belongs to no one but the state; one who tills empty land possesses it. (Vigasin and Samozvantsev 1985, 107) We learn a lot from this passage in Kautilya. First, there certainly was land—probably a considerable amount—that the crown owned or at least controlled. Second, most farmers had something like a lease for life and paid taxes to the government. Later in the *Arthashastra*, we learn that the normal tax on the land was one sixth of the crop, but that it might be as high as one fourth or even one third or one half on very fertile land, or even lower than one sixth on land that is difficult to farm. (A.2.15.3, 122; A.5.2.2, 296) Third, we know this crown land was not "owned" by the individual farmers, because the state could seize the land if the farmers were not productive. Finally, Kautilya clearly thought in terms of incentives; he wanted productive farmers on land difficult to cultivate to be encouraged, and he thought it fair to vary the tax rate according to the fertility of the land.

In another passage on taxes we discover that once more Kautilya saw fairness and justice as good policy. For example, "The king should exempt from taxes a region laid waste by the army of an enemy or by foresters, or afflicted by disease or famine." (A.2.1.36, 58) In addition, the state is there to promote agriculture and help farmers. "And he should favor them with grains [seeds], cattle and money. These they should pay back afterwards at their convenience. And he should grant to them favours and exemptions which would cause an increase in the treasury, (but) avoid such as would cause loss to the treasury." (A.2.1.13-15, 56) State promotion of agriculture included state funding of irrigation. "He should cause irrigation works to be built with natural water sources or with water to be brought in from elsewhere." (A.2.1.20, 57) Moreover, the Director of Agriculture should collect and make available "seeds of all kinds of grains, flowers, fruits, vegetables, bulbous roots, roots, creeper fruits, flax and cotton." (A.2.24.1, 148)

The state must also store food and other items for times of calamity. In discussing the building of a fortified city, Kautilya made a long list of what to store that included fats and grains, dried vegetables and dried meat, perfume—he was never one to miss out on his allocated allotment of pleasure—and poison, wood, weapons, and so on. And he added that the official in charge "should cause the old to be constantly replaced by the new." (A.2.4.27-28, 71) Similarly, in outlining the tasks for the Superintendent of the Magazine and the Director of Agriculture, Kautilya enumerated seemingly countless foods and provisions and concluded, "From these [the Superintendent of the Magazine] should set apart one half for times of distress for the country people, (and) use the (other) half." (A. 2.15.22, 1-21, 124) Finally, "during a famine, the king should make a store of seeds and foodstuffs and show favour (to the subjects), or . . . share (his) provisions (with them)." (A.4.3.17, 263) So much is the king responsible for his subjects, Kautilya advised that if the kingdom ran short of provisions, the king should try to move with the population to other land, seek shelter with an ally, or entrust the kingdom to a new king. (A.4.3.18-19, 263-64)

Kautilya also urged the king to have a policy of settling new lands "by bringing in people from foreign lands or by shifting the overflow (of population) from his own country." (A.2.1.1, 55) He sought to found new villages "consisting mostly of Shūdra agriculturalists and sometimes prisoners of war who became slaves working new land, with a minimum of one hundred families and a maximum of five hundred families." (A.2.1.2, 55; see Mookerji 1988, 124-32, and Sharma 1990, 160-61; Thapar 1987, 9)

Kautilya wanted the state to subsidize these new settlements. The king "should provide one making a new settlement with grains, cattle, money and other things." (A.5.2.4, 297) Once more we find the image of the king or the government as the kindly father taking care of children. "He should, like a father, show favours to those whose exemptions have ceased." (A.2.1.18, 56) In advocating a benevolent and caring state planning for the general good and for the benefit of the treasury, Kautilya recognized that there was no conflict of interest between prosperous small farmers and the financial health of the state.

Did the king or the state—which, as Thapar points out, were not clearly distinguished in Mauryan times (Thapar 1997, 64-65) and as Choudhary indicates, Kautilya himself regarded the king as the state (Choudhary 1971, 47)—own all of the land? The consensus among historians is that in addition to crown lands there was private ownership of land. Historians point to three points made in the *Arthashastra*. First, Kautilya clearly stated that some land could be sold by one citizen to another. "Kinsmen, neighbours and creditors, in this order, shall have the right to purchase landed property (on sale). After that, others who are outsiders (may bid for purchase)." (A.3.9.1-2, 219) This passage clearly implies private ownership, although *perhaps* someone leasing land for life from the state is just transferring this lease to another for a price. Second, Kautilya maintained that the state should make grants of lands to certain people for the benefit of the state. "He should grant (lands) to priests, preceptors, chaplains and Brahmins learned in the Vedas (as) gifts to Brahmins, exempt from fines and taxes, with inheritance passing on to corresponding heirs, (and) to heads of departments, accountants and others, and to *gopas* [heads of five or ten villages], *sthānikas* [revenue officers], elephant-trainers, physicians, horse-trainers and couriers, (lands) without the right of sale or mortgage." (A.2.1.7, 56) This passage clearly implies that Brahmins would receive the right of private ownership, although others who receive grants of land could not sell or mortgage that property, and as a result, their "ownership" was only partial. Finally, when Kautilya declared, as we saw above, that one should not take away land that was hard to farm from one who was making it productive, some interpret him as saying that the prospect of genuine ownership would help to settle lands difficult to cultivate. (Saletore 1975, 466-67)[1]

As I mentioned above, scholars remain divided on this issue of land ownership. Kulke and Rothermund apparently agree with Megasthenes that the king or the state owned the land, and Basham says that in ancient India, "the majority of thinkers on the subject favored the doctrine of royal ownership [of land]." (Kulke and Rothermund 1991, 62; Basham 1963, 111) By contrast, without offering any evidence, Bhargava states flat out that "the idea of the whole state being the property of the king was unknown to Indian tradition," (Bhargava 1996, 82) a sentence he seems to have copied word for word from Sastri, [Sastri 1996e, 177]) and Sharma asserts that, "evidence for royal ownership of land in ancient times is weak." (Sharma 1991, 80) Sastri may approach an answer as well as we can so many centuries later in saying that the king had an "interest in the land" and that he "controlled and regulated the use of land," but that these practices fell short of full ownership. (Sastri 1996e, 177) In his exhaustive study, Saletore maintains, "Kautilya clearly refers to two types of land within the State: one variety belongs to the king and the other to private persons." (Saletore 1975, 466; see also Sen 1967, 12) Thapar makes the most sense in reminding us that India was so vast that, "it is in fact impossible to maintain that one particular type of land ownership existed, " and therefore Mauryan India must have had a variety of types of land use and ownership. She concludes, "State ownership of land did not exclude individuals from owning small areas of cultivable land, which they could cultivate themselves with a little assistance. It merely means that small-scale ownership was not the dominant feature." (Thapar 1997, 63, 65; see also, Thapar 1987, 9-10)

If a nation is to have a large treasury that sustains a huge bureaucracy—and Wolpert maintains that Chandragupta's "army of spies, soldiers, and civil bureaucrats . . . probably totaled more than a million men" (Wolpert 1982, 58)—there must be taxes, and Kautilya focused on taxes at length. Revenue from leasing lands was of course central to his system of taxes, but he mentioned many other kinds of taxes, as well. The main sources of revenue were taxes on land, taxes on irrigation water provided to farmers, income from state-owned mines, taxes for the use of forests, income from allowing herds to graze on royal land, and duties and imposts on trade. (A.2.6.1, 75) Kautilya also discussed in detail revenue from what he called "the fort," that is, daily life behind the walls of the city. "Custom-duties, fines, standardization of weights and measures, the City-superintendent, the mint master, the superintendent of passports, spirituous liquors, animal slaughter, yarn, oil, ghee, sugars, the goldsmith, the market-establishment, prostitutes, gambling, buildings, the group of artisans and artists, the temple-superintendent, and what is to be received at the gates and from outsiders—these constitute (the source of income called) 'fort.'" (A.2.6.2, 75) Because the government con-trolled so much in the economy, Kautilya could expect revenue from taxes on prostitutes and on alcohol, leasing buildings and issuing passports, and so on.

Kautilya thought that he could fix in a fair manner, once and for all, these sorts of taxes. To offer some examples, those who dealt in gold, silver, diamonds, horses, or elephants would pay a tax of fifty *panas*. (Elephants were extremely valuable in ancient India. Arrian noted, "Nor do the Indians consider it any disgrace to a woman to grant her favour for an elephant, but it is regarded as a high compliment to the sex that their charms should be deemed worth an elephant." [McCrindle 1960, 227]) Those who dealt in cloth, copper, medicine, and wine would pay forty *panas*; major artisans would pay a tax of twenty *panas*. "Actors and prostitutes shall pay half their wage." (A.5.2.23, 17-20, 298) Kautilya understood that fair taxation would build popular support for a king, and that onerous burdens of taxes would make a king unpopular and perhaps the victim of a rebellion, and thus tax rates should be fixed according to one's ability to pay. (Sen 1990, 133) The king "should take from the kingdom fruits as they ripen, as from a garden; he should avoid unripe (fruit) that causes an uprising, for fear of his own destruction." (A.5.2.70, 301) Once more, social justice and self-interest coincided.

When we examine industry under the Mauryan economy, we find a great deal of nationalization of industry, something like state socialism, but also considerable private industry and commerce on a small scale. (Mookerji 1988, 102, 203) The modern reader is astonished at how far this nationalization went, and it shocks us to see a sentence such as this: "Fisherman shall pay one-sixth (of their catch) as rent for the boats"! (A.2.28.3, 162) Just think what this means. Not only did the state own and apparently manufacture the boats for fishermen, but there had to be a state bureaucracy to take one-sixth of the catch each day and turn it into more durable wealth for the state. Just as extraordinary, Kautilya saw the Director of Trade and the Superintendent of Markets fixing prices for many goods and controlling or watching the prices charged by traders for other goods. (A.2.16.2-3, 127; A.4.2.19, 28-30, 260-61; see Kohli 1995, 78-83)

Most state enterprises discussed by Kautilya are not nearly so startling, and we should emphasize that this kind of state assistance to the economy was not unique to ancient India. (Sarkar 1935, 343-44) The state, for example, apparently had a monopoly on producing weapons. "The Superintendent of the Armoury should cause to be made machines for use in battles, for the defence of forts and for assault on the enemies' cities, also weapons, armours and accoutrements by artisans and artists expert in those lines." (A.2.18.1, 131) Similarly, Kautilya wanted the Superintendent of Chariots to supervise the manufacture of war chariots, training chariots, and chariots for attacking an enemy city. (A.2.33.5, 180) (According to Strabo, "A private person is not allowed to keep either a horse or an elephant," [McCrindle 1960, 90] a fascinating statement that, by the way, stands in conflict with the declaration that a woman was praised if she received an elephant as a result of granting sexual favors to a wealthy man.) Moreover, only the state should make products with gold and precious metals. "The goldsmith should cause gold and silver work of the citizens and country people to be carried out by workshop artisans." (A.2.14.1, 116) After prohibiting any private manufacture of items in gold, Kautilya set penalties for private work in gold ranging from fines to the cutting off of the fingers of one hand. (A.2.14.11-14, 117-18) Once more delving to the details, Kautilya even mandated that the Superintendent of Gold should build a gold workshop "with a court-yard having four work-halls without intercommunication (and) with a single door"! (A.2.13.1, 110) Not surprisingly, if the state controlled the use of precious metals, then the state also controlled the mines, and indeed mining was, in Kautilya's eyes, a vital source of income. Said Kautilya, "the treasury has its source in the mines." (A.2.12.37, 110) He proposed a Director of Mines who was "conversant with the science of (metal) veins in the earth and metallurgy." (A. 2.12.1, 105) Kautilya also sought to appoint a Salt Commissioner who would supervise salt works, although Kautilya recognized that some salt would be imported with a tariff of one-sixth the salt's value, and he even implied that, if licensed, private businesses might collect and sell salt. (A.2.12.28-34, 109-10)

Whereas the Director of Metals "should establish factories" for copper, lead, brass, bronze, steel, iron, and other metals, he should also "(establish) trade in metal-ware." (A.2.12.23, 108) To make certain that trade in these and other items was reliable, the state was responsible for manufacturing and circulating accurate weights and measures. "The Superintendent of Standardisation should cause factories to be established for the manufacture of standard weights and measures." (A.2.19.1, 134) The state also apparently controlled trade, judging the worth of imports and levying tariffs and promoting trade abroad. (Mookerji 1988, 102) In settling new lands, the state should loan to farmers "grains, cattle and money" and provide pastures for cattle and irrigation for farms. (A.2.1.13, 14-20, 56-57) Because Megasthenes reported that there was no private banking system for borrowing and lending money, (McCrindle 1960, 72) we can reasonably conclude that the state took over banking practices.

The state took over other industries to promote the general moral well-being of the population. Whereas it does not appear as if the state had a monopoly on the production of alcohol, it did take control of distributing it by setting up government owned alehouses, the only places where citizens could legally drink. The Controller of Spirituous Liquors "should cause alehouses to be built," (A.2.25.11, 154) and this not only controlled and limited the consumption of wine, but also facilitated the jobs of spies and informers because they could frequent the state-run alehouses and talk freely to subjects. (On rare occasions private individuals could make alcohol. "On the occasion of festivals, gatherings and fairs, permission to manufacture and sell liquor should be granted for four days" [A.2.25.36, 156]). In a similar fashion, the state controlled the vice of gambling. "The Director of Gambling should cause gambling to be carried on in one place." (A.3.20.1, 250) Although Kautilya did not declare that all courtesans would be in one place in a city, he did envision state control of courtesans who would be licensed by the state and pay a tax to the state. Each courtesan "shall communicate (to the Superintendent [of Courtesans]) the payment, the gain and the (name of the) man." (A.2.27.24, 161) Sures Chandra Banerji notes that Kautilya not only tolerated these "immoral practices" of drinking, gambling, and sexuality, but he was happy to use these "unethical" means in order to control and to tax the people, again providing for the well-being of the state. (Banerji 1993, 187, 301-2)

In addition, the state took over some manufacturing for humanitarian reasons, for example, to employ those who could not find regular jobs. "And those women who do not stir out—those living separately, widows, crippled women, or maidens—who wish to earn their living should be given work." (A.2.23.11, 147) N. N. Law observes that Kautilya's welfare state policies—irrigation works, highways, waterways, dams, bridges, planting flowers and trees, cultivating medicinal plants, and so on—all amounted to a full-scale public works program. (Law 1914, 2-3)

Reading about Kautilya's proposed economy is like encountering some strange combination of Hobbes, Madison, Hegel, and Foucault: Hobbes, because Kautilya assumed that all would try to maximize power and self-interest; Madison, because he thought that a science of politics could check and channel such self-interest; Hegel, because once the science of politics was operating the government officials would have no choice but to look after the common good; and Foucault, because Kautilya foresaw a world where everyone watched everyone else, power was omnipresent, and one's best friend might be an unwitting and unwilling informer. Nevertheless, Kautilya emphatically thought his economy would work for the general good. Over and over he stated that state ownership or control of the economy was for the benefit of the subjects, and if there was one class this Brahmin mistrusted and disliked, it was the class of traders and merchants who acted on selfish greed. Kautilya even hinted, in a passage that reminds one of Aristotle, that much property should be for common use. "For one not rendering help in a common dwelling, for one obstructing a thing used in common and in case of prevention of (rightful) use (by others), twelve *panas* is the fine. Double that (is the fine) for destroying (what is used in common). Of sheds, courtyards and latrines, of fireplaces and pounding sheds, and of all open (spaces), use in common is desired." (A.3.8.26-28, 218) Cooperative ventures such as wells, irrigations, and building roads were part of each village, and Kautilya expected all villagers to do their share of the work. (Nagarajan 2 1992, 78) Kohli is correct in saying that Kautilya's "economy was to be based on justice geared to peoples' needs," (Kohli 1995, 15) and Choudhary rightly concludes that Kautilya had "a romantic view of the state" in which, if each does his or her duty, the state will invariably help "every individual in realising his [and her] own end." (Choudhary 1971, 157)

## Notes

1. For a discussion of details on ownership of land, see Samozvantsev 1984.

# Chapter 5

## FOREIGN POLICY AND WAR

As a political realist, Kautilya assumed that every nation acts to maximize power and self-interest, and therefore moral principles or obligations have little or no force in the interactions among nations. While it is good to have an ally, the alliance will last only as long as it is in that ally's, as well as one's own, self-interest. "An ally looks to the securing of his own interests in the event of simultaneity of calamities and in the event of the growth of the enemy's power." (A.8.1.59, 389) Whether one goes to war or remains at peace depends entirely upon the self-interest of, or advantage to, one's kingdom. "War and peace are considered solely from the point of view of profit." (Nag and Dikshitar 1927, 15) One keeps an ally not because of good will or moral obligation, but because one is strong and can advance the self-interest of the ally and because the alliance is advantageous to one's country. "When one has an army, one's ally remains friendly, or (even) the enemy becomes friendly." (A.8.1.56, 389) Because nations always act in their political, economic, and military self-interest, that means even times of peace have the potential to turn abruptly into times of war, allies into enemies, and even enemies into allies. Stein notes correctly that Kautilya was describing a foreign policy, not of a great empire like that of the Mauryas, but of small warring states in incessant conflict, such as India experienced before the Mauryan empire. (Stein 1998, 78) Kautilya probably assumed that peaceful empires cannot last forever, and conflict among smaller states is more common in history.

## Principles of Foreign Policy

Kautilya is most famous for outlining the so-called mandala theory of foreign policy in which one consider's one's immediate neighbors as one's enemies, but regards any state on the other side of a neighboring state as an ally; put bluntly, the enemy of my enemy is my friend. Imagine a series of states to one's west, and then number them starting with the oneself; states numbered 1, 3, 5, 7, and so on will likely be friends, whereas states 2, 4, 6, 8, and so on will probably be one's enemies. (One can do the same thing with concentric circles, which would look more like a mandala, but I think it is difficult to envision these circles as states.) Kautilya put this basic principle in a number of different ways. Most simply, "One with immediately proximate territory is the natural enemy." (A.6.2.19, 318) Elsewhere he stated this mandala theory of foreign policy in more detail. "With respect to the middle king [he himself], the third and the fifth constituents are friendly elements. The second, the fourth, and the sixth are unfriendly elements." (A.7.18.1, 380) And in one paragraph, he used the image of a wheel. "Making the kings separated by one (intervening territory) the felly and those immediately proximate the spokes, the leader should stretch himself out as the hub in the circle of constituents." (A.6.2.39, 320)

For Kautilya, this principle of foreign policy—that nations act in their political, economic, and military self-interest—was a timeless truth of his science of politics or *arthashastra*. It is not that nations never act in a humanitarian or altruistic manner—indeed, Kautilya advocated numerous humanitarian acts that also coincided with one's self-interest—it is just that one must assume, if one is entrusted with political or military power, that one's neighbors will eventually act in their own interests, or put another way, one would be betraying one's own people if one did not assume a worst case scenario. A nation forced to rely on the kindness of one's neighboring states is weak and, unless it can change rapidly, doomed to destruction. One can see this same assumption in the work of Thucydides who was writing history about a century before Kautilya and in the thoughts of the Chinese legalist Han Fei Tzu who wrote about fifty years after.

Kautilya assumed that he lived in a world of foreign relations in which one conquered or suffered conquest. He did not say to himself, "Prepare for war, but hope for peace," but instead, "Prepare for war, and plan to conquer." Diplomacy is just another weapon used in prolonged warfare that was always either occurring or being planned for. Notice how he analyzed one's own unique configuration of potential enemies and allies, and then coldly concluded how one must think and act. "The king, endowed with personal excellences and those of his material constituents, the seat of good policy, is the would-be conqueror. Encircling him on all sides, with territory immediately next to his is the constituent called the enemy. In the same manner, one with territory separated by one (other territory) is the constituent called the ally." This much just repeats the principles of foreign policy we discussed above, but then notice how Kautilya believed that we must regard neighboring states. "A neighboring prince possessed of the excellences of an enemy is the foe; one in calamity is vulnerable; one without support or with weak support is fit to be exterminated; in the reverse case, fit to be harassed or weakened. These are the different types of enemies." (A.6.2.13, 318)

Offering an excellent discussion of Kautilya's mandala theory of foreign policy, G. P. Singh continues by correctly stating that this is ancient India's most notable contribution to political theory. (Singh 1993, 115-30, esp. 127; see also, Law 1931b, 464-74, and 709-15; and Law 1932, 54-63) Although Singh analyzes Kautilya's theory well, he makes a mistake in labeling Kautilya's mandala theory of foreign policy an argument based on the doctrine of balance of powers, because Kautilya was not offering a modern balance of power argument. In the nineteenth and twentieth centuries, international relations theorists have defended the doctrine of balance of powers, because equally armed nations will supposedly deter each other and therefore no war will result. We do find this argument occasionally in Kautilya. "In case the gains [of two allies of equal strength] are equal, there should be peace; if unequal, fight." (A.7.6.3, 338) Or, "the conqueror should march if superior in strength, otherwise stay quiet." (A.9.1.1, 406) Whereas theorists of international relations suggest that a nation arm itself so that it can ensure peace, Kautilya wanted his king to arm the nation in order to find or to create a weakness in the enemy and conquer, even to conquer the world, or at least the subcontinent of south Asia. In reading his *Arthashastra*, we find no moral considerations; rather, we discover merely what Kautilya regarded as the nature of power. The king "should march when by marching he would be able to weaken or exterminate the enemy." (A.9.1.44, 408) And Kautilya assumed that every other state would act in a like manner. "And even the equal who has achieved his object tends to be stronger, and when augmented in power, untrustworthy; prosperity tends to change the mind." (A.7.5.47, 337) Just as Thucydides, Kautilya regarded a request for negotiations as a sign of weakness, indeed the last desperate act of a nation trying to survive. "A weaker king may bargain with a stronger king with the offer of a gain equal to his troops, when he is in a calamity or is addicted to what is harmful [that is, women, wine, or gambling] or is in trouble. He with whom the bargain is made should fight if capable of doing harm to him; else he should make the pact." (A.7.7.7, 343)

Whereas Clausewitz said that war is just an extension of domestic politics, (Keegan 1993, 3-24) Kautilya argued that diplomacy is really a subtle act of war, a series of actions taken to weaken an enemy and gain advantages for oneself, all with an eye toward eventual conquest. A nation's foreign policy always consists of preliminary movements toward war. "In this way, the conqueror should establish in the rear and in front, a circle (of kings) in his own interest, with the excellences of the constituent, called the ally. And in the entire circle, he should ever station envoys and secret agents, becoming a friend of the rivals, maintaining secrecy when striking again and again. The affairs of one, who cannot maintain secrecy, even if achieved with particular success, undoubtedly perish, like a broken boat in the ocean." (A.7.13.42-44, 366) In Kautilya's foreign policy, even during a time of diplomacy and negotiated peace, a king should still be "striking again and again" in secrecy.

Consider some of the measures Kautilya supported during times of peace. If opposed by an alliance of nations, a king should secretly "sow dissensions" within the alliance (A.7.14.2, 366) until one or more of the parties in the alliance becomes weak. When he has weakened a neighbor, the king "should violate the treaty." (A.7.14.7, 367) Or, in another example, "The wise (conqueror), making one neighboring king fight with another neighboring king, should seize the territory of another, cutting off his party on all sides." (A.7.6.15, 339) For Kautilya, two kinds of kingdoms confront any king—those weak kingdoms fit to be exterminated and those strong kingdoms that, over a long period of time, one can only secretly harass and hope to weaken. "As between an enemy fit to be harassed and an enemy fit to be exterminated, acquisition of land from an enemy fit to be exterminated is preferable. For, the king fit to be exterminated, being without support or with a weak support, is deserted by his subjects when, on being attacked, he wishes to flee taking with him the treasury and the army." (A.7.10.26-27, 354) (When Kautilya wrote of "exterminating" an enemy, he meant only to kill the rulers, and, as we will see in more detail later, he thought the best policy toward ordinary citizens was to treat them well and recruit them.) Best of all is to attack an enemy that is "disunited," rather than an enemy in which the subjects have organized themselves into "bands." (A.7.11.18, 356) During times of peace and negotiations, Kautilya wanted spies and secret agents to exploit the divisions within a country. Most countries, he maintained, have four kinds of unhappy subjects—the enraged, the frightened, the greedy, and the proud. Secret agents can widen and deepen these divisions by inciting these four types of people to act against their king.

"And he should win over the seducible in the enemy's territories by means of conciliation and gifts and those not seducible by means of dissension and force." (A.1.13.12, 1-11, 32)

Because a king abides by a treaty only for so long as it is advantageous, Kautilya regarded all allies as future conquests when the time is ripe. For example, "That ally who remains common to the enemy (and himself), he should divide that rogue from the enemy (and) when divided, exterminate him, thereafter (exterminate) the enemy." (A.7.18.36, 383) Kautilya also sought to take a nation trying to remain neutral or "indifferent" and secretly provoke war between that nation and a neighboring kingdom, until the neutral nation sought his help, and Kautilya's king could "place him under (his) obligations." (A.7.18.37, 383) Kautilya himself had no moral qualms about breaking obligations or trust. "That ally who might do harm or who, though capable, would not help in times of trouble, he should exterminate him, when trustingly, he comes within his reach." (A.7.18.40, 383) In the *Mahābhārata*, a diplomat advises a king, "Carry your enemy on your shoulders as long as it is necessary; when the right moment arrives, dash him down to pieces." (Indra 1957, 80)

Foreign policy is just an extension of a nation's wars, and foreign policy is not there to end wars, but rather to ward off defeats and to make sure one is successful in warfare. For Kautilya, all ambassadors were potential spies with diplomatic immunity. (Majumdar 1960, 64) Indeed, Kautilya put in his *Arthashastra* an entire section about how to "fight with the weapon of diplomacy." (A.12.2, 462; see Indra 1957, 80-81)

## War

Kautilya thought there was a "science" of warfare, presumably part of his larger science of politics. The Commandant of the Army, he suggested, should be "trained in the science of all (kinds of) fights and weapons, (and) renowned for riding on elephants, horses or in chariots." (A.2.33.9, 180) Just as Machiavelli advised his prince to attend to matters of warfare constantly, so did Kautilya advise the king not to leave military matters entirely in other hands. "Infantry, calvary, chariots and elephants should carry out practice in the arts outside (the city) at sun-rise. . . . The king should constantly attend to that, and should frequently inspect their arts." (A.5.3.35-36, 304) Just as the king's agents spied on officials in the state bureaucracy, so too must the king have spies to assess the loyalty of soldiers. What greater threat is there to a king than having a military coup remove him from power? "And secret agents, prostitutes, artisans and actors as well as elders of the army should ascertain with diligence, the loyalty or disloyalty of soldiers." (A.5.3.47, 305)

Kautilya wrote a startling sentence in his section on foreign policy. "Of war, there is open war, concealed war and silent war." (A.7.6.17, 339; see Indra 1957, 8-9; Dhar 1981, 89-90) Open war is obvious, concealed war is what we call guerilla warfare, but silent war is a kind of fighting that I do not believe any other thinker has discussed. Silent war is a kind of warfare with another kingdom in which the king and his ministers—and unknowingly, the people—all act publicly as if they were at peace with the opposing kingdom, but all the while secret agents and spies are assassinating important leaders in the other kingdom, created divisions among key ministers and among classes, and spreading propaganda and disinformation. "Open war is fighting at the place and time indicated; creating fright, sudden assault, striking when there is error or a calamity, giving way and striking in one place, are types of concealed warfare; that which concerns secret practices and instigations through secret agents is the mark of silent war." (A.7.6.40-41, 342) In silent warfare, secrecy is paramount, and, from a passage I quoted earlier, the king can only prevail by "maintaining secrecy when striking again and again." (A.7.13.43, 366) This entire concept of secret war was apparently a new and original idea with Kautilya. (Majumdar 1960, 63)

Open warfare, Kautilya declared, is "most righteous," (A.10.3.26, 440) but he was willing to use any and all kinds of warfare to achieve consolidation and expansion of the kingdom. There is no question of morality here—other than the general good of one's kingdom—but only of strategy. "When he is superior in troops, when secret instigations are made (in the enemy's camp), when precautions are taken about the season, (and) when he is on land suitable to himself, he should engage in an open fight. In the reverse case, (he should resort to) concealed fighting." (A.10.3.1-2, 438) How different all this is from the image of war, certainly exaggerated, found in the *Mahābhārata* or the *Rāmāyana* in which the central figure is the great hero in the regal chariot who frightened all before him. (Majumdar 1960, 29)

In Book 12, Kautilya outlined the situation in which one's own kingdom is weak and is thus about to be attacked by a stronger king. He maintained that, "there are three kings who attack: the righteous conqueror, the greedy conqueror and the demoniacal conqueror." (A.12.1.10, 460; see Nag and Dikshitar 1927, 28) Whereas one can easily satisfy a righteous conqueror simply by submitting to his rule, one must surrender "land and goods" as well as money in order to satisfy a greedy conqueror. The demoniacal conqueror, however, will stop only after he has seized "land, goods, sons, wives and life." (A.12.1.11-16, 460) (Kautilya apparently saw himself as advising a righteous conqueror, although he did want some tribute from defeated peoples.) A weak king must give up anything if it is inevitable, but he must find a way to survive to fight another day. "He should preserve his body, not wealth; for, what regret can there be for wealth that is impermanent?" (A.12.1.32, 462) Kautilya did not advocate giving in to a conqueror without countermeasures, among which were: the king should use "diplomatic or concealed warfare," attempt to conciliate his enemy with gifts, direct secret agents to wield "weapons, poison or fire" to destroy the enemy's fort or camp, instruct secret agents to promote a coup by a "pretender from his family or a prince in disfavour," send the demoniacal king listless elephants that had been poisoned, give to the enemy king treasonable or alien troops, surrender to an entirely different king and give him all but the capital city, have secret agents instigate a revolt among the subjects of the enemy king, "employ assassins and poison-givers," use an astrologer to persuade a "high officer" of the enemy king to try a coup, command secret agents to declare that the Regent of the king is about to take power and have secret agents kill leaders at night and blame it on the Regent of the enemy king, use secret agents in the countryside to protest oppression of the enemy king's bureaucracy and kill agents of the king hoping to start a revolt, or finally set fire to palaces and stores of grain and blame this on the Regent to the enemy king. (A.12.17-32, 461-62; A.12.2.8-33, 462-64; see also, Law 1931a, 258)

Most intriguing, Kautilya advocated using women as weapons of war. Kautilya certainly regarded women as a source of satisfaction for troops at war. When setting up camp for the army, "courtesans (should be encamped) along the highways." (A.10.1.10, 434) And Kautilya certainly saw women as an addictive source of pleasure, worse than wine or gambling, that a good king must enjoy only in moderation. "Deliverance is possible in gambling, without deliverance is addiction to women. Failure to show himself, aversion from work, absence of material good and loss of spiritual good by allowing the right time to pass, weakness in administration and addiction to drink (result from addiction to women)." (A.8.3.53-54, 395) Precisely because women are such a powerful addiction, the king can use them against an enemy. For example, if a king is trying to undermine a ruling oligarchy, he "should make chiefs of the ruling council infatuated with women possessed of great beauty and youth. When passion is roused in them, they should start quarrels by creating belief (about their love) in one and by going to another." (A.11.1.34-35, 457) A woman supposedly in love with one leader should go to another, profess her love for him, and urge him to murder the first leader. "Then she should proclaim, 'My lover has been killed by so and so.'" (A.11.1.37, 39, 457) Obviously such tactics create mistrust among leaders of an oligarchy and also bring about the death of key enemies. In the chapters about how a weak king can stave off disastrous conquest by a stronger king, Kautilya again turned, as just one possible tactic among many, to women as weapons of war. "Keepers of prostitutes should make the (enemy's) army chiefs infatuated with women possessed of great beauty and youth. When many or two of the chiefs feel passion for one woman, assassins should create quarrels among them." (A.12.2.11-12, 463) Secret agents can destroy high officers in the enemy army either with poison or with "love-winning medicines." (A.12.2.14, 463)

Speaking of justice to an enemy about to conquer is the last tactic of the weak, just as Thucydides showed in his recreation of the debate about Melos. In Thucydides's *The Peloponnesian War*, written just before 400 B.C.E., or a century before Kautilya's *Arthashastra*, the Melians try to talk about justice and fair play when facing the prospect of conquest by the Athenians, but the Athenians contend that such arguments are the last, desperate tactic of those facing defeat. "Since you know as well as we do," said the Athenians to the Melians, "that, when these matters are discussed by practical people, the standard of justice depends on the equality of power to compel and that in fact the strong do what they have the power to do and the weak accept what they have to accept." (Thucydides 1972, 402) After that both the Melians and the Athenians debate only what is in the self-interest of Athens. Similarly, willing to try all tactics, even desperate ones, Kautilya made up a powerful speech to give to the king about to conquer, a speech offering a mixture of moral exhortation and arguments based on the self-interest of the conqueror. In this speech, Kautilya depicted an envoy saying to the conquering king that he should accept a treaty and "pay regard to [his] spiritual and material well-being," that conquering a kingdom willing to surrender on reasonable terms is an "impious act," that it is not in the conquering king's self-interest since, "to fight with brave men who have given up all hope of life is a rash deed" and the conqueror will lose troops and "material good," that such a conquest will only unite his enemies all the more, that the conquering king's enemies are only waiting for him to be weakened in order to attack, that he himself is risking death, that war itself in which men on each side die is "an impious act," and that he should not listen to "enemies masquerading as friends" who are giving him false advice as to his real self-interest. (A.12.2.1-7, 462) In much the same way as Thucydides, only more dramatically, Kautilya demonstrated the realities of diplomacy and war as well as the ineffectiveness of moral pleas when confronted with conquest by the more powerful.

In writing about waging a war, Kautilya made a striking statement that clearly separates him, at least in one way, from Machiavelli. "For, the destruction of an enemy's forces is principally dependent on elephants." (A.7.11.16, 356; see Srivastava 1985, 80-81) As I have shown earlier, the treasury is most valuable in raising an army, procuring equipment, and entering a war. After the treasury and the army, Kautilya focused on the importance of the fort. "Dependent on the fort are the treasury, the army, silent war, restraint of one's own party, use of armed forces, receiving allied troops, and warding off enemy troops and forest tribes. And in the absence of a fort, the treasury will fall into the hands of enemies. For, it is seen that those with forts are not exterminated." (A.8.1.38-40, 388) (A mountain fort is more valuable than a river fort, because it "is easy to protect, difficult to lay siege, difficult to climb." [A.7.10.33, 355])

Kautilya was inconsistent in ranking the importance of the treasury, the army, and the fort, because it seems that Kautilya occasionally regarded the people—a popular army—as the most important of all. As he put it, "one should seek a fortress with men." (A.7.15.11, 370) Well before Machiavelli defended a republican army, well before Mao defended a people's war as invincible, Kautilya urged the king to be popular with the people and rely on the countryside. "If weak in might, [a king] should endeavor to secure the welfare of his subjects. The countryside is the source of all undertakings; from them comes might." (A.7.14.18-19, 368) The "undertakings" of the fort, the treasury, and the army all depend ultimately on the people of the countryside. "Bravery, firmness, cleverness and large numbers are (found) among the country people." (A.8.1.29-30, 387) Kautilya here was cautiously making a revolution in warfare, relying not quite as much on the warrior class of Kshatriyas. The *Dharmasūtras*, which preceded Kautilya, urged an army of Kshatriyas, and in an emergency, also Brahmins and Vaishyas. Kautilya had no use for Brahmin troops—"by prostration, an enemy may win over Brahmana troops"—but he liked the energy, numbers, and strength of Shūdras. (A.9.2.21-24, 412; Sharma 1990, 173-74) His praise of ordinary men from the lower two *varnas* was unusual in ancient India. "As between land with the support of a fort and one with the support of men, the one with the support of men is preferable. For, a kingdom is that which has men. Without men, like a barren cow, what could it yield?" (A.7.11.23-25, 357) Says Sharma, "Kautilya alone holds that the army made up of vaisyas and sudras is important." (Sharma 1990, 237) Kautilya apparently believed that an army of Kshatriyas was best; (A.9.2.24, 412) warriors were supposed to find their "highest duty and pleasure" by dying in battle, and Arrian—again relying on Megasthenes—suggested that as much as one fifth of the population under Chandragupta's empire were warriors or Kshatriyas. (Das 1994, 143-44) In addition, Kautilya clearly argued that sections of the army should consist "mostly of persons from the same region, caste or profession."

(A.9.2.9, 411) Using a little common sense, we can see that he is suggesting that men of an army should know one another, that an army of friends fighting side by side is the most difficult to defeat. For example, where should the king be during battle? "A bare army, without standards, consisting of warriors related as fathers, sons and brothers, should be the place for the king. An elephant or a chariot should be the vehicle for the king, guarded by calvary." (A.10.3.39-40, 441) (Kautilya wanted a man who deceptively looked like the king to head the army. [A.10.3.42, 441])

And thus, a king's power, for Kautilya, is in the end tied to the power and popular energy of the people, without which a king can be conquered. "Not being rooted among his subjects, [a king] becomes easy to uproot." (A.8.2.18, 392) Although Kautilya wrote of using money to raise an army and even of "purchasing heroic men," (A.9.1.7, 406) he was not advocating mercenaries who fought only for pay, but he was merely outlining the cost of paying, supplying, and feeding soldiers. "Hereditary troops are better than hired troops." (A.9.2.14, 412) In other words, troops composed of men born in the kingdom and thus loyal to the king since birth are better than strangers fighting for money, as Machiavelli noted so often later. It is not at all clear, remarked Kautilya, that "inviting alien troops with money" (A.9.7.10, 428) is an advantage or a disadvantage.

## Waging War

In Kautilya's view of the world, expansion by a prosperous kingdom was inevitable, natural, and good, and as a consequence, moral considerations—other than what was for the good of the kingdom—did not enter into his deliberations. "When in decline as compared to the enemy, he should make peace. When prospering, he should make war. (When he thinks) 'The enemy is not able to do harm to me, nor I to him,' he should stay quiet." (A.7.1.13-15, 321) Kautilya repeated this same point frequently. "The conqueror should march if superior in strength, otherwise stay quiet. . . . [A king] should march when by marching he would be able to weaken or exterminate the enemy." (A.9.1.1, 44, 406, 408) In short, if one can win, then one should go to war. As Kangle says, the *Arthashastra* "preaches an ideal of conquest." (Kangle 1992, 263)

On the questions of whether and when to wage war, Kautilya did not urge ethical deliberations, but rather prudent and careful calculation. If calamity has struck an enemy, if the subjects, "harassed by [an enemy king's] own army or disaffected with him, are easy to entice, being weakened, without energy or divided among themselves; the enemy has his draught-animals, men, stores and fortifications reduced in consequence of fire, floods, disease, epidemic or famine, then he should make war and march." (A.7.4.15, 332-33) When weakness appeared in a neighboring kingdom, a king should attack. As Rajendra Prasad says, Kautilya believed that "whenever an enemy king is in trouble, and his subjects are exploited, oppressed, impoverished and disunited, he should be immediately attacked after one proclamation of war." (Prasad 1989, 58-60) Every adjacent kingdom should be looked upon as an enemy and classified; if a kingdom is strong, Kautilya called it a "foe"; if a kingdom is suffering calamity, then it is "vulnerable"; if a kingdom has weak or no popular support, then "it is fit to be exterminated." Even if one cannot attack a strong neighbor or "foe," one can harass it silently and weaken it over time. (A.6.2.16, 318) What Kautilya called an enemy "fit to be exterminated" was an enemy with little or no popular support, an enemy whose subjects quite likely would desert to Kautilya's attacking army. (A.7.10.26-27, 354) It is also quite clear, and I am just repeating for emphasis what I said earlier, that Kautilya was emphatically not urging a massacre of enemy troops and civilians, but rather he sought to defeat and kill the leaders of an enemy kingdom, recruit what troops he could, incorporate this new land and its people into his kingdom, and "plunder his grains, cattle and cash." (A.7.4.7, 332) And Kautilya argued, or perhaps assumed, that imperial expansion was the correct goal. "After conquering the enemy's territory, the conqueror should seek to seize the middle king, after succeeding over him, the neutral king. This is the first method of conquering the world. . . . And after conquering the world he should enjoy it divided into *varnas* and *āśramas* in accordance with his own duty." (A.13.4.54-55, 62, 490-91)

In Kautilya's mind, treaties were agreements between kingdoms of roughly equal power, agreements a king should break if they are no longer advantageous, and thus, believing that a treaty will provide a wall of protection against a strong enemy would be a foolish act. If an ally with whom a king has a treaty becomes weakened, that is, if the treaty is no longer to a king's advantage, then the king "should violate the treaty." (A.7.14.7, 367) Or, "When after making a pact he intends to violate it, . . . he should demand a gain not received or more." (A.7.8.8, 347) Because Kautilya thought that promises or agreements were strategies and not moral obligations, he had no moral qualms about violating a promise. "The commander of a frontier fort, by offering the surrender of the fort, should get part of the (enemy's) troops inside and destroy *when full of trust*." (A.12.5.25, 472, my emphasis) To protect his own people, a king has an obligation to weaken or destroy any potential enemy. "That ally who might do harm or who, though capable, would not help in times of trouble, he should certainly exterminate him, *when trustingly, he comes within his reach.*" (A.7.18.40, 383, my emphasis) Drekmeier is certainly correct in saying that, "In outlining military campaigns Kautilya disregards the traditional humanitarian principles laid down to regulate the conduct of war." (Drekmeier 1962, 212) In an unrealistic, moralizing passage in the *Dharmasūtras* that Kautilya most certainly ignored, the authors directed that a king should not "strike with barbed or poisoned weapons"! (*Dharmasūtras,* 159) In Book 9, Kautilya listed various "hindrances to gain"; among them were pity, piousness, and "regard for the other world." (A.9.4.25, 419) In short, in waging war, compassion and morality and religious principles have no place.

In another way, moral considerations did enter into Kautilya's calculations; whereas it is best to wage war against an unjust king who has no public support, it is wise to avoid war with a righteous king whose subjects will fight energetically on his behalf. Kautilya noted that if one has a choice about where to attack, it is always best to attack an unjust kingdom. "The subjects help the king who is justly behaved. . . . Therefore, [a king] should march only against [an enemy] with disaffected subjects." (A.7.5.10-11, 334; Nag and Dikshitar 1927, 18) Once more, morality is sometimes advantageous and in one's self-interest. "The unjustly behaved [king] would cause even settled land to be laid waste." (A.7.11.31, 358) By being unjust, a king loses all popular support, thereby weakening the kingdom and rendering it easily conquered. "The king fit to be exterminated, being without support or with weak support, is deserted by his subjects when, on being attacked, he wishes to flee taking with him the treasury and the army." (A.7.10.27, 354) If a king has a choice of attacking a strong king who is unjust or a weak king who is just, he should actually attack the stronger king, because the stronger king's subjects, weary of injustice, will not help the more powerful king and might even join the war against him. (A.7.5.16-18, 335) An unjust state is really two states, already at war with one another, the rulers and the ruled, the strong and the weak, the rich and the poor. (Deb 1938, 370) Kautilya paused to remind a king how practical it was to be just toward his subjects. "Subjects, when impoverished, become greedy; when greedy they become disaffected; when disaffected they either go over to the enemy or themselves kill the master. Therefore, [a king] should not allow these causes of decline, greed and disaffection among the subjects to arise, or, if arisen, should immediately counter-act them." (A.7.5.27-28, 335) A domestic political policy of social justice is, in the long run, the best defense against outside enemies. "For, one attacking a righteous king is hated by his own people and by others, one attacking an unrighteous king is liked (by them)." (A.7.13.12, 362; Nagarajan 2, 1992, 165)

Kautilya maintained that a humanitarian policy toward a defeated people was practical. If a king massacres those whom he has defeated, then one frightens all those kingdoms that surround him and even terrifies his own ministers. (A.7.16.30-31, 375) Rather, one gains more land and new and loyal subjects if one treats the defeated in a magnanimous manner. Certainly a conquering king must silently kill those former leaders loyal to the defeated king, but those who approach him promising loyalty should be treated generously. "He should not use towards them insults, injuries, contemptuous words or reproaches. And after promising them safety, he should favour them like a father." (A.7.16.22-23, 374) Because a conquering king intends to expand his territory and acquire new subjects, he must treat a defeated people well. "After gaining new territory, he should cover the enemy's faults with his own virtue, his virtues with double virtues. He should carry out what is agreeable and beneficial to his subjects by doing his own duty as laid down, granting favours, giving exemptions, making gifts and showing honour." (A.13.5.3-4, 491) Indeed, the conquering king should "order the release of all prisoners and render help to the distressed, the helpless and the diseased." (A.13.5.11, 492) It is sound military policy to "establish a righteous course of conduct." (A.13.5.14, 492) What is moral is once more practical. Just as one can kill a traitor, but cannot use force "against a multitude of people," (A.9.6.2-5, 422) so one can kill the leaders of a defeated kingdom, but must bring the great majority of the citizens peacefully into one's own kingdom. In this instance, Kautilya was following traditional advice given in the *Dharmasūtras*. "Āryas condemn the killing of those who have thrown down their weapons, who have dishevelled hair, who fold their hands in supplication, or who are fleeing." (*Dharmasūtras,* 53; see also, *Laws of Manu,* 137-38) And by these actions, Kautilya fulfilled his own definition of a righteous conqueror who sought glory and the submission of the enemy, but not greedy pillaging or lawless killing. (Krishna 1996, 96)

Kautilya demanded much of his soldiers, because they had to be brave and fierce in battle, but gentle and kind toward those whom they had defeated. "When attacking the enemy's fort or camp, they should grant safety to those fallen down, those turning back, those surrendering, those with loose hair, those without weapons, those disfigured by terror and to those not fighting." (A.13.4.52, 490) After a king has subdued the country and taken care of the people, he should "grant safety to the countryside," settle subjects down to farm the land, and "induce" even those who had fought against him to settle down and farm (even by giving tax exemptions!), all because the countryside needs farmers and the new kingdom wants prosperity. "For, there is no country without people and no kingdom without a country," meaning a prosperous—not a ravished—countryside. (A.13.4.2-5, 485-86)

Both Sun Tzu (c. 400-320 B.C.E.) and Machiavelli, in books entitled *The Art of War,* pointed out that a general should always give an enemy the hope of escape and never surround a nearly defeated enemy completely.[1] Enemy soldiers who have hope of living will eventually run for safety, and then they are easily killed, but soldiers surrounded with no choice but to fight or die will fight with an unimagined ferocity. Kautilya was arguing something similar. Let the enemy soldiers know that the king will be generous in victory, will allow defeated soldiers to return to their land, and will take no reprisals except against the leaders of the opposing kingdom. "But against the leaders among them, he should act as in 'the infliction of (secret) punishment.'" (A.9.6.5, 422) After such humanitarian policies toward the defeated populace have become widely known, ordinary enemy soldiers will surrender in great numbers. By contrast, if a king announced that he would massacre every soldier, then all would fight to the death. Said Kautilya, "The vehemence of one returning again to the fight and despairing of his life becomes irresistible; therefore, [a king] should not harass a broken enemy." (A.10.3.57, 442) Similarly, "to fight with brave men who have given up all hope of life is a rash deed." (A.10.2.4, 462)[2]

A conquering king should reassure a defeated people that not much, except their rulers, will change. The king who has triumphed "should adopt a similar character, dress, language and behavior (as the subjects). And he should show the same devotion in festivals in honour of deities of the country, festive gatherings and sportive amusements." (A.13.5.7-8, 491) He should keep his promises, especially to those who helped him win, he should honor the local "deities," and he should make grants of land and money to men distinguished in wisdom and piety. (A.13.5.11,6, 491-92) And the conquering king should show his goodwill toward the defeated by instituting "a righteous custom, not initiated before." (A.13.5.24, 493) While the victorious king is reassuring the general population with generous policies, he must continue to kill anyone who is dangerous and those who are disgruntled. "He should put down by silent punishment those capable of injuring or those brooding on the master's destruction." (A.13.5.17, 492) In what might be a surprising observation about those whom the king has killed, Kautilya commented that if one must kill a dangerous person, the king must leave his property untouched. "And he shall not covet the land, property, sons or wives of the slain one." (A.7.16.26, 374) Kautilya had the same insight into human emotions that Machiavelli had nearly eighteen hundred years later. Said Machiavelli, "And when [the prince] is obliged to take the life of any one, . . . he must abstain from taking the property of others, for men forget more easily the death of their father than the loss of their patrimony." (Machiavelli, Ch. 17) A king becomes hated more readily for taking the property that belongs to a family than for killing the head of the family.

Kautilya was ready to use almost any means of violence in fighting a war, although he wanted his king to direct his violence at the leaders of the opposing king and not toward ordinary people. For example, Kautilya discussed at length how to use poison, but the use of poison was almost always directed at key enemy commanders. For example, "giving unadulterated wine to the army chiefs, [the secret agent] should give them (wine) mixed with poison when they are in a state of intoxication." (A.12.4.6, 467) Whereas Kautilya did suggest that an army laying siege to a fort try to "defile the water," (A.13.4.9, 486) this seems to be a measure designed to make those in the fort surrender from illness, not a measure to kill everyone in the fort. Mostly, Kautilya addressed the question of how to assassinate a king—by hiding "inside the image of a deity or a hollow wall" and emerging at night, by making something heavy fall on the king, or by use of women as secret agents to "drop on him serpents or poisonous fire and smoke." (A.12.5.43-48, 473) Kautilya was willing to use any possible means to assassinate an enemy king—drown him, burn him with fire, suffocate him with smoke, even use crocodiles as assassins, not to mention women and children as poison-givers. (A.12.4.22-28, 9-10, 468-69) The wonder of assassination, according to Kautilya, is that it is so efficient. "For, an assassin, single-handed, may be able to achieve his end with weapon, poison and fire. He does the work of a whole army or more." (A.9.6.54-55, 425) Kautilya was willing to let loose on the enemy "persons who have committed great crimes" who could use "weapon, poison and fire." (A.9.6.34, 424) Kautilya was also willing to use these same measures of assassination against the leaders of rebellious subjects in his own kingdom, (A.9.5.14-15, 421; A.5.6.14, 48, 310, 313; A.1.18. 14, 45) although sometimes the king must put down a rebellion with troops. (A.9.3.9-14, 414)

Aside from assassination, another method used to defeat an enemy without full scale battle was to arrange for the enemy to quarrel and fight itself. We have already seen how Kautilya intended to use beautiful women to instigate fights among high officers or officials. If the promise of pleasure can ignite quarrels, so can the promise of power. Arrange for a secret agent, disguised as an astrologer, to tell a high officer that he has all the marks of a king, and similarly arrange for a female secret agent, the wife of this officer, to complain that the king wants to take her into his harem. A third secret agent who is a cook or a waiter should lie, saying that the king has ordered him or her to poison the high officer. "Thus with one or two or three means, [the king] should incite the high officers one by one to fight or desert [the enemy king]." (A.12.2.24, 19-23, 463-64) In a discussion about sowing dissensions among oligarchies, Kautilya suggested that "assassins should start quarrels by injuring objects, cattle or men at night" and that assassins "should stir up princelings enjoying low comforts with (a longing for) superior comforts, and that "assassins should start quarrels among the followers of the chiefs in the oligarchy by praising the opponents in brothels and taverns." (A.11.1.14, 9, 8, 455) Once again, women are a weapon. After a beautiful woman has stirred the desires of two men, she can urge the murder of one by saying the first is harassing her and how much she loves the second. Afterwards, "she should proclaim, 'My lover has been killed by so and so.'" (A.11.1.39, 34-38, 457) The goals were constantly to "sow discord" and to foment and inflame "mutual hatred, enmity and strife." (A.11.1.6, 455)

Much of this advice violated the tacit code of war found in the great Indian epics and the many law books. The assassination of envoys and the use of poison were considered against the rules of warfare and thus not honorable. "Fighting in battle, [the king] should not kill his enemies with weapons that are concealed, barbed, or smeared with poison or whose points blaze with fire." (*Laws of Manu,* 137) Such a contrast with Kautilya! (A.13.4.1-24, 485-88; see also, Srivastava 1985, 32) Spies were common in Indian history (*Laws of Manu,* 141, 143-44, 151, 225-30) but not spies who assassinated enemy officials and started quarrels among enemy leaders. (Majumdar 1960, 40-41, 65, 36) An excellent book on warfare in ancient India discusses spies, but does not mention secret agents who carried out assassinations. (Srivastava 1985, 101) Once more Kautilya judged the means by the result, and the result he sought was the general good of his kingdom.

Another military tactic that Kautilya praised was what we now call disinformation or propaganda designed to demoralize or frighten enemy soldiers. For example, secret agents should appear as messengers to troops saying, "'Your fort has been burnt down or captured; a revolt by a member of your family has broken out; or, your enemy or a forest chieftain has risen (against you).'" (A.10.6.48-50, 453) After spreading the rumor that the Regent or a high administrator of the enemy king has announced that the king is in trouble and may not come back alive and thus people should take wealth by force and kill their enemies, secret agents should kill and steal at night, trying to cause civil upheaval. "When the rumour has spread far and wide, assassins should rob citizens at night and slay chiefs, (saying at the time), 'Thus are dealt with who do not obey the Regent.'" Then they should put bloody evidence in the Regent's residence. (A.12.2.26, 25-28, 464) Again, secret agents should spread rumors, always in a confidential manner, that the king is furious with such and such a leader, and then these agents should assassinate key leaders. "And to those who have not been slain, secret agents should say, 'This is what we had told you; he who wants to remain alive should go away.'" (A.12.3.4, 465) Kautilya was especially fond of the tactic of utilizing disinformation to flatter a second or third son and thus persuade him to try a coup against his own family. (A.12.3.15, 466) Convinced that disinformation could also inspire his own troops, Kautilya wanted agents to announce fabricated victories to his own troops, while proclaiming fictitious defeats inflicted on the enemy. "On the occasion of a night-battle, [secret agents] should strike many drums, fixed beforehand as a signal, and announce, 'We have entered it; the kingdom is won.'" (A.12.4.21, 469; Srivastava 1985, 89)

Much of this disinformation made use of religion. Placed strategically, astrologers "should fill [the king's] side with enthusiasm by proclaiming his omniscience and association with divine agencies, and should fill the enemy's side with terror." (A.10.3.33, 440) Once more the needs of the state must always be primary, and the king commands religion to serve the state. "He should make (Brahmins) recite blessings invoking victory and securing heaven." (A.10.3.36, 440) Singers and poets should "describe the attainment of heaven by the brave and the absence of heaven for cowards." (A.10.3.43, 441) Secret agents who have infiltrated the enemy side should use animal blood in order to "cause an excessive flow (of blood) from honoured images of deities," and then interpret that as a sure sign of future defeat for the enemy. (A.13.2.27, 479) Kautilya wanted anyone was associated with religion or superstition—"soothsayers, interpreters of omens, astrologers, reciters of *Purānas*" and so on (A.13.1.7, 475)—to proclaim to his own troops and to the enemy the king's "association with divinities" or "his meeting with divinities," (A.13.1.1, 8, 474-75) creating confidence on his own side and simultaneously misgivings and even terror among enemy soldiers. Those priests in charge of interpreting omens must make certain that dreams and other signs are always favorable to the king's efforts and unfavorable to the enemy. (A.13.1.9, 475) Every kind of superstition can be useful, (Sharma 1954, 225-28) and for Kautilya religious authorities must be for hire.

In addition to brave and well-equipped soldiers, warfare requires deception, and over and again Kautilya advocated the above measures and more for deceiving both his own and the enemy troops. If caught behind enemy lines, Kautilya outlined ways for one to escaped by disguise—"in the disguise of a heretical monk," "decked out as a corpse," or "wearing a woman's garb." (A.12.5.38-40, 472) And he was eager to use multiple and varied means to fool and to terrify the enemy. "He should strike terror in the enemy with machines, by the employment of occult practices, through assassins slaying those engaged in something else, by magical arts, by (a show of) association with divinities, through carts, by frightening with elephants," and so on. (A.10.6.48-50, 453) A favorite tactic in battle was to pretend to be defeated, retreat in apparent disorder, and then attack a disorganized and unsuspecting enemy. "Or, feigning a rout with treasonable, alien and forest troops, he should strike at the (pursuing enemy when he has) reached unsuitable ground." (A.10.3.1, 438) At all times, Kautilya wanted his king to use deception, play roles, and create appearances. Why risk heavy losses or even defeat in battle if deception and assassination can weaken or even defeat the enemy? Even if a king is forced to surrender in order to survive, Kautilya wanted him to pretend that his surrender was "an excellent thing" until he was clever or strong enough to fight back. (A.7.15.29, 372) Warfare was violent, but it also called for one who could calmly create false impressions, like a poker player in the deadliest of games.

## Notes

1. "To a surrounded enemy you must leave a way of escape. . . Show him there is a road to safety, and so create in his mind the idea that there is an alternative to death. . . Wild beasts, when at bay, fight desperately. How much more is this true of men! If they know there is no alternative they will fight to the death. (Sun Tzu, 109-10)

"It is necessary, above everything that has been mentioned, to be careful not to bring the enemy into utter despair. About this Caesar was careful when fighting the Germans; he opened a road for them, seeing that since they could not run away necessity was making them bold." (Machiavelli, 700)

2. John of Plano Carpino, a contemporary of Genghis Khan, described one of his tactics this way: "If it happens that the enemy fight well, the Tartars make a way of escape for them; then as soon as they begin to take flight and are separated from each other they fall upon them and more are slaughtered in flight than could be killed in battle." (Chaliand 1994, 469)

# Chapter 6

# POWER, ADVANCEMENT, AND A THEORY OF HISTORY

In European history and in the Judeo-Christian tradition, thinkers usually accepted either a cyclical theory of history or a linear view of history. Plato, Polybius, Cicero, Machiavelli, and Rousseau all embraced various different cyclical theories of history in which a city-state, a nation, or a culture rises, reaches some peak of perfection and then declines, decays, and perhaps dies, although it might start the cycle again. In Book 8 of his *Republic*, Plato outlined a cycle of history in which his republic—in truth an aristocracy, or rule by the best—is followed by timocracy, oligarchy, democracy, and tyranny. Just as all living things go through a cycle of life and death, so do states, "since for everything that has come into being destruction is appointed." (Plato, 546a) Most of these thinkers with a cyclical view of history seemed to look upon states as they looked upon the biological world of plants and animals, that is, just as all living things grow, decay, and die, so do political entities, and all great statesmen can do at certain moments in history is slow down the rate of decline and decay, a conviction held, for example, by Cicero. Borrowing from Plato, Aristotle, and Polybius, Cicero stated, "For there is a remarkable rotation and, if I may say so, cycle of changes in the life of states. It is the business of the philosopher to understand the order in which these changes occur." (Cicero 1976, 134) In Cicero's view, the cycle followed a predictable pattern. "The government is thus bandied about like a ball: tyrants receive it from kings; from tyrants either to aristocrats or to the people; and from the people to oligarchs or tyrants. The same form of government is never long retained." (Cicero 1976, 150-51) For Cicero, the peak of "political wisdom" for a statesman was to discern the nature of decline and "be able to retard the movement or forestall it." (Cicero 1976, 178) In particular, he thought that a constitutional government that mixed elements of monarchy, aristocracy, and democracy would slow the cyclical decline, although it could not prevent it. Once a nation or a culture has passed, other cultures, some better and some worse, will rise to take its place. In these cyclical views, history repeats itself, that is, nations go through similar stages, attain similar kinds of greatness, and undergo similar kinds of decay and decline.

The Hebrew *Bible* gave us the first linear view of history, a conviction that history defines itself by unique, nonrepeatable events. For example, there will never be a Garden of Eden again, a flood in which Noah saved humankind and nature, another exodus from Egypt, another covenant with Moses, and so on. After the nation of Israel had fallen away from its covenant with God, prophets such as Amos, Jeremiah, and Isaiah began to say that, just as history had a clear beginning in the Garden of Eden, so was God promising a grand culmination of history if the Hebrew people would turn back and observe the covenant with God. Despite the fact that Israel was a "sinful nation" (Isaiah 1:4) that was rightly being punished for rejecting God, Isaiah—speaking the words of the Lord—said that if the people of Israel became "willing and obedient," (Isaiah 1:19) if they would "cease to do evil, learn to do good, seek justice, correct oppression, defend the fatherless, plead for the widow," (Isaiah 1:16-17) then they could look forward to a new and lasting order of justice and righteousness. "He shall judge between the nations, and decide for many peoples; and they shall beat their swords into ploughshares,. . . neither shall they learn war anymore." (Isaiah 2:4) Indeed, God promised that a new "government will be upon his shoulder," (Isaiah 9:9) and the dispersed Hebrews would be united with Jerusalem once more as their capital. (Isaiah 1:11-12, 16)

All of this became even more starkly clear with the Christian tradition and its eschatological promises, such as a second coming of Jesus Christ and a day of judgment. Once more, history was viewed as linear with a beginning, a middle, and an end, and always a clear purpose and goal. In Matthew, Jesus spoke of a day of judgment. "The angels will come out and separate the evil from the righteous, and throw them into the furnace of fire; there men will weep and gnash their teeth." (Matthew 13:49-50) Revelations promises a judgment, the rule of Christ for a thousand years, and then a new heaven and a new earth in which God "will wipe away every tear from their eyes, and death shall be no more, neither shall there be mourning nor crying nor pain any more, for the former things have passed away." (Revelations 20:21:4, 20:4-6, 21:1) With this, of course, the history of the earth would end.

These linear views of history enjoyed a secular rebirth in the seventeenth and eighteenth century as liberal thinkers began to speak of progress and revolutionary thinkers began to paint pictures of a future golden age. With the European invention of the printing press—China had invented this first—and with European exploration of the world, and finally, with European scientists such as Copernicus, Galileo, and Newton, it became harder to argue that history was the same familiar story repeated again and again, and it became easier to suggest that history was composed of unique, nonrepeatable events. And just maybe history was pointing toward something better and more grand, some goal or purpose or destiny for humankind. This certainly became the view of defenders of progress such as Condorcet, Kant, Hegel, and Mill, and it was an essential assumption of revolutionaries as widely different as Cromwell, Robespierre, and Marx. Condorcet was perhaps the best representative of the Enlightenment faith in human progress, a progress that would be simultaneously moral, intellectual, scientific, and technological. "The perfectibility of man is truly indefinite; and [the] progress of this perfectibility . . . will doubtless vary in speed, but it will never be reversed." (Condorcet 1979, 4)

Kautilya implicitly embraced a theory of history very different from anything in the European tradition. This struck me most forcefully when I started to think about Kautilya's science of politics, a science good for all times and places, a timelessly valid science, much like Hobbes had put forth what he regarded as a science of politics or theorems of politics that would be forever valid as is Euclid's geometry. I realized this when I understood that Kautilya believed that the wages, not to mention the occupations, for government officials to be exactly the same in a thousand years—48,000 *panas* for a Crown Prince, 24,000 *panas* for the Treasurer, 4000 *panas* for the Superintendent of Elephants, 2000 *panas* for a Grade II courtesan, 500 *panas* for a village level poisoner, and so on. (Rangarajan 1992, 289-92) In attempting to set salaries once and for all that were "proper and just," Kautilya was trying to ignore "market conditions." (Sen 1967, 102-3, 107-8) So too were the taxes paid to the state timeless amounts, except for periods of emergency. When Kautilya stated that "dealers in gold, silver, diamonds, gems, pearls, corals, horses, and elephants shall pay a tax of fifty [*panas*]," (A.5.2.17, 298) he apparently was setting this forth as a scientific principle, good for all time. Similarly, Kautilya both "feared' and "opposed" allowing prices to rise and fall with supply and demand. (Sen 1967, 32) And when he discussed the "science of building," (A.2.3.3, 61-62; A.10.1.1, 433) he apparently thought that these principles of building—and I assume even the materials for building—would not change.

When Kautilya discussed time, and like Hobbes he wanted clear definitions for his science of politics, he gave the state the responsibility for measuring time and space, and he offered a rather traditional view of seasons. (A.2.20, *passim*, 138-41) Thinkers focusing on the change and repetition of seasons often move to a cyclical view of history, but Kautilya did not. Late in his *Arthashastra*, he returned to the notion of time in an intriguing passage. "Time is of the nature of cold, heat and rain. Its various parts are: night, day, fortnight, month, season, half year, year and *yuga*. In them, he should start work that would augment his own strength." (A.9.1.22-24, 407; see Sarma 1991, 185-88) This passage tells us clearly that time is the arena in which a king prepares to advance toward his political and military goals, but by referring to *yuga*, Kautilya places his world in a Hindu framework of time that Europeans have difficulty in comprehending. According to Hindu thought as expressed in the *Purānas*, the world goes through a cycle of four ages or *yugas*, from a perfect *krta* age of 1,728,000 years in which all follow their duties or *dharma* to a dark age or a *kali* age, of only 432,000 years—our own age—in which almost all have fallen away from *dharma*. According to *The Laws of Manu*, in the perfect *krta* age, people "are free from sickness, achieve all their goals, and (have) a lifespan of four hundred years." (*Laws of Manu,* 12) By contrast, in the *kali* age, according to the *Mahānirvana Tantra*, "Now the sinful Kali Age is upon them, when Dharma is destroyed, an Age full of evil customs and deceit." (Brown 1958, vol. 1, 19) When the four ages of progressive decline have passed, a total of 4,320,000 years, a new perfect age begins, and this gigantic cycle starts anew. The total period of four ages or *yugas* is called a *manvantara*. After 1000 *manvantaras*, which is but one day for Brahma, the universe will be destroyed after which the universe will experience one night of Brahma which is again 1000 *manvantaras*. One day and one night of Brahma constitute about 8.6 billion years, and the process repeats itself for all eternity. As Gavin Flood puts it, "there is no end to this process; nor purpose other than the Lord's play." (Flood 1996, 113, also, pp. 112-116; also, Frauwallner 1993, vol. 1, 90-93; Balslev 1983, 145-47; and Embree 1988, 220-21) Hopkins discusses this view of time found in the *Vishnu Purāna*, and concludes that the creator Vishnu engages in creation as sport, playing with Spirit, Time, and Matter. After one of these long cycles of history, some 8.6 billion years, then, "When Vishnu again decides to play, the process begins anew." (Hopkins 1971, 101) (Lipner insists that this sport and play of the gods is responsible, as seen for example in the fact that the gods make certain that the laws of justice and *karma* persist. [Lipner 1994, 254-55]) Mircea Eliade adds to this. "A hundred of these 'years' of Brahma, or

311,00 billion human years, constitute the life of the god. But even this considerable life-span of Brahma does not exhaust Time, for the gods themselves are not eternal and the cosmic creations and destructions go on forever." (Eliade 1992, 103)[1]

The civilizations built by men and women over centuries seem but an insignificant instant in this time perspective. (Eliade 1992, 105) In one sense, of course, this is a cyclical view of history, but the cycles are so gigantic that human beings can scarcely fathom them, much less incorporate them into their lives. Because these cycles are beyond comprehension, and because Indian philosophies have tried to escape from human time, which is invariably a realm of suffering, Indian political thought has in reality been "ahistorical." (Lannoy 1992, 419) In a fascinating recent article, Roy W. Perrett has argued that most ancient Indian thinkers did not regard the study of history as important because it was not the kind of knowledge that would bring *moksa* or liberation, which is indeed an escape from human history. (Perrett 1999, 320-21)

## A Pendulum Theory of History

With such an enormous scope of time, it is impossible to apply either a cyclical or linear view to politics. So what theory of history is implicit in Kautilya's writing? I call it a pendulum theory of history, because Kautilya depicted a kingdom as passing through three phases—decline, stability, and advancement—back and forth, ceaselessly. For example, if a king should find himself weak, he should seek shelter and prepare himself and his subjects "to progress from decline to stable condition and from stable condition to advancement." (A.7.1.36, 324; Nagarajan 2 1992, 153) His science of politics can help weaken or exterminate enemies and thus prolong one's time in the state of advancement, but unfortunately mistakes and natural calamities always occur to transport a kingdom back from advancement to decline. "He, who is well-versed in the science of politics, should employ all the means, viz., advancement, decline and stable condition as well as weakening and extermination. . . . [Such a king] plays as he pleases, with kings tied by the chains of his intellect." (A.7.18.43-44, 384) In general, "Of decline, stationary condition and advancement, he should seek to attain each later one in preference to each earlier one." (A.9.7.51, 430) (After this last passage, Kautilya admitted that, for political and strategic reasons, one might decide to postpone advancement.)

What is advancement? A time in which a king "shall be able to promote [his] own undertakings concerning forts, water-works, trade-routes, settling on waste land, mines, material forests and elephant forests, and to injure these undertakings of the enemy." (A.7.1.20-21, 322) In general, "When in decline as compared to the enemy, [a king] should make peace. When prospering, he should make war." (A.7.1.13-14, 321) Choudhary asserts, "To Kautilya, human affairs appeared to be in a state of constant flux, and a state must either expand or decline." (Choudhary 1971, 243)

What causes decline? A king brings about decline by acting in an unjust and greedy fashion toward his subjects until they become disenchanted and want to rebel or revolt. "By discarding the good and favouring the wicked," "by discontinuing customary practices that are righteous," by "suppression of piety," "by seizing those who ought not to be seized and not arresting those who ought to be seized," by failing to stop thieves, by destroying material well-being and creating poverty, and so on, a king brings decline. (A.7.5.19-26, 335) Using Kautilya's *Arthashastra*, a king can remedy these injustices and reverse this decline. "Therefore, he should not allow these causes of decline, greed and disaffection among the subjects to arise, or, if arisen, should immediately counteract them." (A.7.5.28, 335) In some sense decline and advancement are linked to prosperity. "Smallness of profit and excess of expenditure is decline, advancement in the reverse case; equality of income and expenditure in undertakings should be known as the stable condition for himself." (A.7.12.30, 361)

In one passage, Kautilya wrote as if this pendulum swinging from decline to stability to advancement and back again was a zero sum game in which the advances of one king were always at the expense of another king. "The flourishing of an enemy's undertaking is decline for the leader, advancement is the reverse case; when the course of undertakings is equal, that should be known by the conqueror as his own stable condition." (A.7.12.29, 361) In another passage, Kautilya apparently concluded that some nations, perhaps those that are not enemies, can advance together. If an advancement "bears an equal fruit (for both) [kingdoms], [the king] should make peace." (7.1.23, 322) At any rate, a king's job is to use Kautilya's *Arthashastra* to bring about advancement and to know how to protect the kingdom in decline, but as history goes—not forward and not around—this pendulum will continually swing back and forth between advancement and decline.

In a book of Jain philosophy called *Pravacanasara* by Kundakunda, the author said, "the quality of time is to roll on." (Embree 1988, 79) Smith notes that the passing of time in Hindu thought is likened to the turning of a wheel, (Smith 1994, 173) Prasad says a common early Indian view was that time is "everflowing like a river," (Prasad 1992, 6) Lipner observes that

Hindus saw time as devouring all things, (Lipner 1994, 251-52) Shyam Gosh remarks that "Hindu philosophy equates death with life," just different modes of consciousness on a space-time continuum whose one characteristic is constant change where all things die and are then reborn, (Ghosh 1989, 1, 208) and Raimundo Pannikar remarks that some in ancient India, "compared time to an ocean where one can see neither the other shore or any island of refuge." (Pannikar 1992, 25) Because the root of the Sanskrit word *kala* or time refers both to counting and to death, (Balslev 1983, 12) it is not surprising to find Krishna in the *Bhagavad Gita* saying both that "of all things that measure I am time" and " I am all-powerful Time that destroys all things." (*Bhagavad Gita*, 86, 92) These images—of time just going, but not going to any place, or time like a wheel that turns but never itself moves forward or backward, or time as bringing death one moment and simultaneously birth—capture Kautilya's implicit assumptions about history well. Time just goes or passes or rolls on or devours. In this arena of time, the king tries to use the science of politics to maximize the moments in which his kingdom is in a state of advancement and minimize periods of decline.

The Buddhist view of time underscores even more dramatically the notion of impermanence. Everything is in constant flux, time brings change that destroys any possibility of something being identical from moment to moment, change that eliminates any possibility of Being. "There is absolutely nothing that remains identical and immutable. Change is total." (Balslev 1983, 16) From instant A to instant B, something X is destroyed or devoured and it becomes something changed into Y, and this holds, under Buddhist philosophies of time, for everything from things to plants to animals to human beings to the universe. "At no two instants can a thing be said to be identical." (Balslev 1983, 80; Rahula 1974, 25) This led obviously to a doctrine, not of a self or soul or *ātman*, but a doctrine of no-self or the absence of a self (*anātman*) that endures from one moment to the next. (Strong 1995, 89) Buddhists claimed that every entity perishes and is replaced by another at every instant, that time does indeed destroy and annihilate, that "there is no room for any notion of unchanging substance." (Balslev 1983, 121, 81, 96) At every moment, Time literally destroys Being and rolls on.[2]

G. R. Malkini outlines one interpretation of the early Indian concept of time that reminds me of the implicit view of time and history in Kautilya. "We have accepted time as beginningless and endless. In such time, progress is followed by regress, so that there is no overall progress towards anything. What is gained is as surely lost or destroyed . . . But in an infinite and beginningless time, all conceivable possibilities must already have been realized, so that nothing new could be brought into existence." (Malkini

1992, 703) Richard Lannoy notes that, "Change does not increase the good," there is nothing new in history, and there is certainly nothing we might call progress. (Lannoy 1992, 418) Or, concludes Eliade, "the world is born, grows weary, perishes, and is born anew." (Eliade 1992, 108) This view of time and history might lead to inaction or passivity; so might the view found in works such as the *Mahābhārata* that time leaves us in the grasp of fate, that life is replete with determinism and preordained events. (Bedekar 1992, 187-91) The notion that all is impermanent can also sometimes "serve as a rationale for apathy." (Lannoy 1992, 417; Puligandla 1992, 409-14) In fact, most in the Indian tradition asserted that we have free will in the face of a time that devours and, over enormous periods, leads to moral decline. (Lipner 1994, 253-54) (Mathura Nath Goswami sees Indian history as linear with a goal of a welfare state whose foundation is *dharma*, but the evidence for this seems very much forced. [Goswami 1994, 2-5])

Agreeing that we have free will and acknowledging that effort is worthwhile, Kautilya seems to view politics like a game to be well played. No grand goal is promised, no culmination of history awaits, and no decline and death of the political order is inevitable, but there is always a new problem or a new configuration of enemies—like the nearly limitless possibilities of pieces on a chess board—that awaits a king and his advisers. Hinduism and Buddhism, with their common wish "for release from the anguish of history, the terror of irreversible time," (Lannoy 1992, 421) seek to escape from history. By contrast, Kautilya was a man who wanted to play the very important game of politics for a long while.

## Notes

1. The Buddhist notion of an eon is comparable to, perhaps even more unfathomable than, the Hindu notion of ages. "If there were a seven-mile high mountain, and once a century it was stroked with a piece of fine cloth, it would be worn away before a great eon would pass. Nevertheless, more eons have passed than there are grains of sand on the banks of the river Ganges!" (Harvey 1990, 33)

2. The philosophy that best paralleled this idea in the ancient Greek world was that of Heraclitus who maintained that everything is "in flux like a river," who saw everything in the world as in perpetual motion like the flames of a fire, and who, according to Plato, declared that one "could not step into the same river twice." (Robinson 1968, 89-91)

# CONCLUSION

In the nineteenth century, French romantic painters journeyed to North Africa, because they could see with their own eyes new colors—in the clothing, in the fruit of the markets, and in the landscapes—not available in Europe. While we may have an idea of the colors of red or blue in our minds, think of the countless variations and shadings of red and blue in the natural and human worlds, a diversity that explodes in more variety as we cross each border. Just as French painters travelled to Algeria to stimulate their imaginations, we read the literature, theology, philosophy, and political thought of cultures beyond the borders of Europe and the United States because they provoke wonder and thought, because they transport us beyond what is customary to us and into realms with new possibilities. We see the world with fresh eyes.

Kautilya is as provocative to one accustomed to European political ideas as any political thinker I know. Some of what he wrote, of course, is unsurprising. A reader understands that Kautilya necessarily wrote political thought constrained by Hindu society including classes, castes, and customs. No thinker in his time or place, not even one as bold and innovative as Kautilya, could imagine ridding India of the four classes or *varnas*—Brahmin priests, Kshatriyas or warriors and rulers, Vaishyas or farmers and merchants, and Shūdras or agricultural laborers—or the system of inherited occupations, subcastes, or *jātis*. Even here, however, Kautilya pushed the edges of this caste system by defending the rights of most Shūdras to be exempt from slavery and by seeking a popular army that relied on Vaishyas and Shūdras. As much as anyone could have done in India at the time, Kautilya defended the status of citizenship for Shūdras. Why did he champion the Shūdras? Because it was in the self-interest of the ruler to have a people's army fiercely loyal to him precisely because the people had been treated justly.

Also, the tradition of kingship was deeply imbedded in the Indian tradition and articulated clearly in law books such as the *Laws of Manu* and the *Dharmasūtras*. Indian tradition said that once long ago there was chaos—no theory of a Golden Age here, in contrast to early China—characterized by what writers called the law of the fishes or a time when the big and strong devoured the small and weak, quite like Hobbes's war of all against all. But then God gave the world kings to bring order. A Hindu state without a king was literally unthinkable, and because a king had earned his power and status through the laws of *karma* and his actions in previous lives, the populace looked upon a king as superhuman, nearly divine. By using punishment, *danda,* or the Rod, in just the right measure—if the king was too severe, he would be hated, and if he was too lenient, he would lose his authority and chaos would ensue—a king brought order and prosperity. Under wise rule, Hindus could pursue the three goals of life—material well-being, spiritual goods, and sensual pleasures. The king himself did his duty or *dharma*, pursued these three goals in life, and lived a life of moderation, avoiding ruinous addictions to women, wine, and gambling.

It is also not suprising to see Kautilya argue that a wise king must take care of his subjects as a father takes care of women and children. Paternalistic in an almost literal sense, Kautilya saw the people of the kingdom not as active citizens but as passive subjects cared for by the king and the state. Arguably the entire notion of a welfare state, in which the state was responsible for those in need either by providing jobs or by supporting those who could not survive without assistance, was first described in the history of political ideas by Kautilya. Moreover, whereas Kautilya did not even entertain the ideas of citizen participation, such as one might find in Greek democracy or the Roman republic, he did describe ways in which a king ascertained the concerns of the populace. By accepting the tradition of the audience hall, one of the most important rooms in the palace at Pataliputra (near modern Patna), Kautilya advised a king to make himself available to "anyone"—one can be skeptical about how many Shūdras or Vaishyas could see the king—who wanted to present an idea or express a grievance. In addition, one purpose of the all-pervasive spying in Kautilya's kingdom was to gather information, that is, public opinion, including who was disaffected and why, so the king could take action before dissatisfaction boiled over into rebellion.

Kautilya's *Arthashastra* stands out in Indian philosophy like a Himalaya mountain on an Oklahoma plain, because the chief concern of Hindus was not politics and power but instead *moksa* or liberation or a union with Brahman that one attains by breaking the cycle of rebirth or *samsāra*. Hindu conquest was a conquest of oneself, so very different from the Greek ideal of glory! As admirable as liberation or *moksa* might be as a goal in life, it is an apolitical or even antipolitical end, and thus leaves comparatively few people speculating about government or politics, which is one reason Kautilya's *Arthashastra* is so distinctive. Amidst so many Hindu writers focusing on *moksa* and *dharma* or one's duty to the divine, Kautilya's book analyzing the pursuit of political power and economics—literally, *artha* or material well-being—is dramatically different, just as is the *Kāma Sūtra* or the study of how to maximize sensual pleasure, which is a perfectly legitimate goal in the life of the Hindu householder, one who is in the second stage of life.

Although any book on politics in ancient India would be unusual, Kautilya startles us even further by providing us with a science of wealth and power and politics to conquer, not our inner selves, but instead the political world. More powerful than elephants or chariots or spears, Kautilya's science is a weapon that can teach a king how to conquer the world up to its four ends, or at least to the natural geographical boundaries of India. Armed with this science, a wise king can toy with his enemies.

It seems plausible that Kautilya was confident, even arrogant, because he and Chandragupta had routed the various Nanda kings, stopped the advances of Alexander's successors, and unified India in empire for the first time. While the *Arthashastra* recounts how that was done, it also advises a king how to proceed with lawful and effective unification, and to accomplish this, Kautilya saw no alternative but a centralized state governing the empire with vast numbers of officials, a bureaucracy looking after the general good, down to the most minute details. In this, Kautilya makes us pause in surprise. Do we want a state this intrusive? Does the state really need to command us to bathe horses twice a day, to wash clothes only on smooth stones, to prescribe penalties for tossing dirt in the road or for harming bushes, and to tell us at what time we must cover our windows at night?

If such detailed regulations seem dangerous and even outrageous, Kautilya's emphasis on economics often makes good sense. If no empire will stay united that is not prosperous, how else could Chandragupta, Kautilya, and the other ministers start new industries and build a system of roads and provide incentives for agriculture but with a centralized state? Perhaps no thinker until John Locke and Adam Smith put such emphasis on the economic prosperity of the country, and no thinker until Hobbes or even

Marx gave such a role to state ownership, intervention, and incentives. Unlike Machiavelli, who seems to argue that an army can feed on the virtues of the armed populace, Kautilya saw a healthy treasury as necessary to give birth to a formidable army. Moreover, a prosperous economy allows individuals the free time to pursue spiritual goals as well.

We don't even have a phrase to describe this economy appropriately, although "socialized monarchy" comes close, and there has been no economy in the world like the Mauryan regimes of Chandragupta, Bindusara, and Aśoka before or since. Imagine a monarchy that perhaps owned, but more likely leased, almost all of the land that was farmed; a monarchy that took upon itself to provide farmers with seeds and information about improved farming techniques; a monarchy that built roads (and planted trees by the roads for shade!) and harbors and took upon itself irrigation projects; a monarchy that owned the mines, the factories for weapons and chariots, factories that made boats for fishermen (who leased them from the state!), and industries that provided most capital and consumer goods; a monarchy that made available work for the unemployed and stipends for the disabled; and a monarchy that ran the alehouses, gambling casinos, and brothels of the country! Finding such ideas in the ancient world is nothing if not provocative. To be frank, we don't know enough about India under the Mauryan kings to know if such practices took place all over the Indian subcontinent or perhaps only in places around the capital. We do know enough from the descriptions of Megasthenes, the Greek ambassador to India, and from the edicts of Aśoka, Chandragupta's grandson, to know that these ideas of Kautilya are at least partly descriptive of the Mauryan Empire and not practices only in Kautilya's imagination.

Because Kautilya detailed the expansive and intricate workings of the state, it is not surprising to find that he offered the first comprehensive theory of the state in what he called the seven constituent elements of the state—the king, his ministers, the countryside, the fortified capital city, the treasury, the army, and the state's allies. Ancient Greek, Chinese, and Roman political thinkers have no comparable theory of the state that includes its purposes and functions. In his *Arthashastra*, Kautilya separates political thinking from theology or political speculation from religious speculation, and it is clear that the Hindu religion—and indeed, all of what Kautilya regarded as superstitions—should be subordinate to the needs of the state. If priestly power bowed to the state, Kautilya also sought to capture the economic power of classes, especially the merchant or business classes, and make them submit to state power.

As much as Kautilya focused on the king, the real power that emerges from his writings is the bureaucracy, the most powerful domestic weapon wielded by the king. In his *Prince*, Machiavelli mentioned only a few advisors to the prince and warned against flattery. By contrast, Kautilya described the jobs of dozens of state and local officials, outlining an elaborate bureaucracy that will carry out the king's will and administer the state for the general good. Kautilya's desired bureaucracy was more extensive than any other found in the ancient world, whether in Egypt, Babylon, Persia, or China. Again, there was no room for democratic citizens. Rather, it is as if the bureaucratic, controlling, and disciplinary nightmare of Weber and Foucault existed not in the modern state but the ancient world, as if Chandragupta's subjects were cared for, but also taught how to think and feel and move, down to the smallest gesture.

Long before Bentham's Panopticon, the circular prison where one guard could watch any prisoner—which became Foucault's symbol for the disciplinary society in which some amorphous authority watches us and trains us down to our most minute movements and phrase—Kautilya sought to establish an elaborate system in which subjects would spy on one another on behalf of authority.

Kautilya trusted no one. The king's family members and closest advisors were tested with bribes, with offers of power, with sexual pleasure with the queen, and so on to see if they were loyal to the king. Surrounded by four circles of guards, the king relied on women who had been raised in the palace and had no family loyalties as his last line of defense. As with any king or tyrant, elaborate precautions were taken against assassination. None of this is unusual. By contrast, one is startled to see Kautilya establish such an extensive network of spies outside the palace. Although it makes sense to spy on places where troublemakers might gather—at alehouses, for example—Kautilya wanted spies in every neighborhood and every village. Whereas Kautilya wished the king to be informed of public opinion so he could address grievances before they became revolts, his use of spies went well beyond ascertaining public opinion. Kautilya wanted to establish omnipresent authority, even the supposed omniscience of the king, so that the population behaved. In short, Kautilya wanted detailed control. The main result from his society filled with spies would be mutual mistrust or mutual suspicion, a situation in which a subject would fear confiding in his or her best friend or even a spouse for fear of being reported, a psychological isolation extending beyond mere loneliness. Although Kautilya genuinely wanted the general good for all, these are the methods of a traditional tyrant.

Add to the presence of spies a huge apparatus for arrest and punishment. Kautilya had no concept of the rights of the accused, in contrast to the Roman republic which was developing the idea of legal rights at just about the same time. In fact, Kautilya goes to great lengths in discussing whom authorities should arrest on suspicion, and he even details how the police should interrogate a suspect. I don't regard Kautilya as a cruel or sadistic person; there seems to be a genuine concern, however odd this may sound, for the accused in his discussions of torture. However, so intent was he on control and setting up his vision of the best possible state that Kautilya was led by the logic of his thinking, maybe by the logic of his controlling personality, actually to discuss when the use of torture is appropriate. It is not surprising to find torture in any state; it has been all too common in every century and on every continent of the world. What is absolutely stunning is to find a political thinker speaking of it openly and reasoning about when it might be used. This is unheard of, I believe, in the history of political thought.

So too is a political thinker continuing at some length about when assassination, sometimes called silent punishment or the weeding of thorns, is appropriate. If the king cannot persuade or trust his enemies, defined immediately as enemies of the state or of the people, then these enemies must be killed. Of course Kautilya was not justifying the killing of any and every dissenter, just those who threatened the king's power, people such as disgruntled ministers, powerful military officers, or even an undisciplined son, or prince, who might ruin the state upon inheriting the throne. Once more, while it does not surprise a reader to discover that assassinations took place in ancient India or anywhere else, it does startle us to see discussions about assassinations in a book of political theory.

Kautilya also discussed the realties of international relations and analyzed the measures needed in warfare in a rare and candid manner. Many scholars see his so-called mandala theory of foreign policy as his finest contribution to political thought. The principle of this theory is straightforward; assume every state bordering on yours is an enemy, and assume every state that does not touch yours but is a neighbor of your enemy is a potential ally. For Kautilya, principles of justice or fairness or the rule of law do not apply in international relations, and if they occur at all, these principles are unusual in practice. Nations act out of political, economic, and military self-interest. If both sides observe a treaty, it is not because of the words on paper and it is not because they believe in justice, but instead the treaty holds because there is a balance of power, because both states are roughly equal in military might. Pleading with an enemy by using fine phrases of justice is only the last resort of the weak; fine words are a country's final, desperate, and—usually—useless weapon. Whereas one can see these ideas in Thucydides' *Peloponnesian War* written about a century before Kautilya's *Arthashastra*, especially in the debates about Mytilene and Melos, Kautilya does more than just observe states acting out of self-interest and elaborates upon a theory of international relations in a detailed and systematic way.

In his theory of international relations, Kautilya startles us once more. What other political thinker repeatedly advises a king to violate treaties whenever those treaties are of no use, whenever a treaty is bothersome to the expansionist plans of the king? In reality, international relations for Kautilya are lawless struggles among those who are strong and those who are weak. Whatever "laws" exist are temporary treaties among those roughly equal, among those who both find peace temporarily beneficial. Diplomatic missions do not serve the cause of peace, but rather they help with the timing of conquest. If one's country is stronger than a neighboring kingdom, a king must attack; if a neighbor suffers a calamity, one must attack; if a treaty is no longer useful, one must attack. And Kautilya believed peace and social justice—and these include the Hindu system of class and caste—were on the other side of successful world conquest. Kautilya wanted Chandragupta, and presumably Chandragupta's son Bindusara and Chandragupta's grandson Aśoka, to bring all kingdoms of the Indian subcontinent into the protective fold of the empire and its governance. Only then could social justice and spiritual well-being prevail.

Kautilya's discussions of warfare are brutally honest. A king must use any and all means to win a war, and Kautilya set forth elaborate discussions of propaganda, disinformation, the use of religion to enhance the morale of his troops and undermine the confidence of opposing troops, the planting of lies to make enemy troops despair or quit, and the frequent use of assassination. In addition, having great confidence in spies and saboteurs, many of whom were women, Kautilya wanted to have opposing generals or ministers or heirs to the throne quarreling amongst themselves over power or the love of beautiful women or anything else that might divide them and thus enable Kautilya's armies to conquer. When Kautilya classified warfare into three categories—open war, concealed war, and silent war—what he wrote was, and perhaps still is, unprecedented. Open warfare is traditional warfare, armies arrayed openly against one another, and concealed warfare is what we call guerilla warfare, attacking and fleeing, harassing an enemy with surprise. Silent warfare involves openly praising another king as a friend and ally, all while striking him again and again with calamity after calamity, assassination after assassination, and quarrel after quarrel among high-ranking officials and officers instigated by spies and saboteurs. The United States would be undertaking silent warfare if its leaders were professing friendship with Mexico while quietly killing key leaders and destroying important aspects of Mexico's defense, all with a long range plan to invade and conquer Mexico. Strike the enemy again and again, said Kautilya, all while openly declaring peace and friendship. Surely this has occurred frequently in the history of warfare, yet who besides Kautilya has talked about it openly?

Assassination? Arrest on suspicion? Torture? Breaking treaties at will? If Kautilya is not an immoral political thinker, then who is? Or maybe it is more complicated than that. Kautilya realized that unifying the warring pieces of India and bringing peace to the subcontinent were dirty undertakings, that homilies about being good and virtuous may well fit times of stability, but not times of crisis that demand daily decisions of life and death. Kautilya was describing the realities of politics—hence the name realist—in times of crisis. The leader who follows traditional morality will bring ruin to himself and his people. And sometimes—not always, but only sometimes, which is the agonizing reality for a political leader—the end does justify the means. While we are taught to reject this notion, we are also taught that the American Revolution—which necessitated the killing of real people—was justified. Kautilya would remind the reader that he didn't create this problem of the political world, but instead he is only telling a leader how to survive and thrive in this political reality. He is telling those who need to know in order to protect their people.

Two more points about Kautilya's moral standards. First, Kautilya observed that it was frequently, perhaps even usually, in the king's self-interest to promote social justice. A king who arrests too many subjects wrongfully, seizes property, raises taxes too high, allows hunger and poverty in his country when it is preventable, and does not provide for the needy or the jobless is likely to come to ruin either by revolt from within or attack from outside by an enemy who will find support among those oppressed. This is why Kautilya warns again and again that a king must be in touch with his people, that he must take care of his people just as a father takes care of his children, and that a king must not be distracted by, or addicted to, wine, women, and gambling. Similarly, in warfare Kautilya did not recommend slaughters or massacres, but instead recognized the wisdom of acting in a humane and generous manner toward defeated soldiers—not their leaders—because these soldiers can become hard-working and loyal subjects. Morality usually enhances self-interest.

Second, like Machiavelli, Kautilya judged political and military actions by results. The survival of the state is of paramount importance, because the state allows individuals to pursue the three goods of life—spiritual well-being, material wealth, and sensual pleasure. Sometimes, more often in times of crisis and rarely in times that are routine, a leader must undertake what are traditionally "evil" actions, such as assassination of domestic enemies or of a foreign enemy leader, to bring about a "good" result. By contrast, to act always in a traditionally "good" way will sometimes bring evil to one's people. And thus the realities of politics demand that we act on political matters with an ethic that we would probably never use with our families and friends and neighbors. But these are the agonizing responsibilities of political leaders. As Max Weber said, anyone who believes that acting in a "good" manner always brings good results and acting in a "bad" way always brings bad results is a political infant. So Kautilya offered his *Arthashastra* or science of politics to those leaders willing to learn, and he saw it as a timelessly valid science that would apply for all times and places. In a sense it was a science of power; one who understood this science was, barring natural disaster, invincible. "He, who is well-versed in the science of politics, . . . plays, as he pleases, with kings tied by the chain of his intellect." (A.7.18.43-44, 384) A king, "though ruling over a small territory . . . conversant with (the science of) politics, does conquer the entire earth, never loses." (A.6.1.18, 317)

# BIBLIOGRAPHY

Agrawal, K. M. 1990. *Kautilya on Crime and Punishment*. Almora, India: Shree Almora Book Depot.

Altekar, A. S. 1962. *State and Government in Ancient India*. 4th ed. Delhi: Motilal Banarsidass.

———. 1995 [1959]. *The Position of Women in Hindu Civilization*. 2nd ed. Delhi: Motilal Banarsidass.

Asthana, Shashi Prabha. 1976. *History and Archaeology of India's Contacts with Other Countries, from the Earliest Times to 300 B.C.* Delhi: B.R. Publishing Corporation.

Ayyar, A. S. Panchapakesa. 1951. *Chanakya and Chandragupta*. Madras, India: V. Ramaswamy Sastrulu & Sons.

Balslev, Anindita Niyogi. 1983. *A Study of Time in Indian Philosophy*. Wiesbaden, Ger.: Otto Harrassowitz.

Bandyopadhyaya, Narayan Chandra. 1927. *Kautilya or an Exposition of His Social Ideal and Political Theory*. Calcutta: R. Cambray & Co.

Banerjea, A. C. 1963. *Studies in the Brāhmanas*. Delhi: Motilal Banarsidass.

Banerji, Sures Chandra. 1993. *Society in Ancient India*. New Delhi: D. K. Printworld.

Basak, Radhagobinda. 1967. *Some Aspects of Kautilya's Political Thinking*. Burdwan, West Bengal, India: University of Burdwan Press.

Basham, A. L. 1963. *The Wonder That Was India*. 2nd rev. ed. New York: Hawthorn Books, Inc.

———. 1990. *The Origins and Development of Classical Hinduism*. Delhi: Oxford University Press.

Basu, Jogiraj. 1969. *India of the Age of the Brahmanas*. Calcutta: Sanskrit Pustak Bhandar.

Bedekar, V. M. 1992. "The Doctrines of Svabhava and Kala in the *Mahābhārata* and Other Old Sanskirt Works," in Prasad, Hari Shankar, ed. *Time in Indian Philosophy: A Collection of Essays*. Delhi: Sri Satguru

Publications. 187-202.

Bhagat, B. 1990. "Kautilya Revisited and Re-visioned." *Indian Journal of Political Science* vol. 51, no. 2, April-June: 186-212.

*The Bhagavad Gita.* 1962. Edited and translated by Juan Mascaro. Baltimore, Md.: Penguin Books.

Bhargava, Purushottam Lal. 1996. *Chandragupta Maurya: A Gem of Indian History.* 2nd rev. ed. New Delhi: D. K. Printworld.

Bhattacharjee, Arun. 1979. *History of Ancient India.* New Delhi: Sterling Publishers.

Bhattacharji, Sukumari. 1994. *Women and Society in Ancient India.* Calcutta: Basumati Corporation.

Bhattacharya, Sibesh. 1984. "Political Authority and the Brahmana-Kshatriya Relationship in Early India—An Aspect of the Power Elite Configuration." *Indian Historical Review* vol. 10, nos. 1-2: 1-20.

Boesche, Roger. 1996. *Theories of Tyranny: From Plato to Arendt.* University Park: Pennsylvania State University Press.

Brown, D. Mackenzie, ed. 1953. *The White Umbrella: Indian Political Thought From Manu to Gandhi.* 2 vols. Berkeley: University of California Press.

Chaliand, Gerard, ed. 1994. *The Art of War in World History: From Antiquity to the Nuclear Age.* Berkeley: The University of California Press.

Choudhary, Radhakrishna. 1971. *Kautilya's Political Ideas and Institutions.* Varanasi, India: Chowkamba Sanskrit Series Office.

Chousalkar, Ashok S. 1990. *A Comparative Study of the Theory of Rebellion in Kautilya and Aristotle.* Delhi: Indological Book House.

Chunder, Pratap Chandra. 1970. *Kautilya on Love and Morals.* Calcutta: Jayanti.

Cicero, Marcus Tullius. 1976. *On the Commonwealth.* Translated by George Holland Sabine and Stanley Barney Smith. New York: Macmillan.

Clarke, J. J. 1997. *Oriental Enlightenment: The Encounter Between Asian and Western Thought.* London: Routledge.

Condorcet, Antoine Nicolas de. 1979 [1795]. *Sketch for a Historical Picture of the Progress of the Human Mind.* Translated by June Barraclough. London: Weidenfeld.

Das, Swaswati. 1994. *Social Life in Ancient India: 800 B.C.—183 B.C.* Delhi: B. R. Publishing Corporation.

Deb, Harit Krishna. 1938. "*The Kautilīya Arthashastra* on Forms of Government." *Indian Historical Quarterly* vol. 14, no. 2, June: 366-79.

Derrett, J. Duncan M. 1973. *Dharmaśāstra and Juridical Literature.* Wiesbaden, Ger.: Otto Harrassowitz.

———. 1976. "*Rajadharma*."*Journal of Asian Studies* vol. 35, no. 4, August: 597-609.

Deshpande, Madhav M. 1993. "Aryans, Non-Aryans, and Brahmanas: Processes of Indigenization." *Journal of Indo-European Studies* vol. 21, nos. 3-4: 215-36.

Deva, Satya. 1984. "State and Bureaucracy in Kautilya's *Arthashastra*." *Economic and Political Weekly* (India), May 12: 811-15.

Dhar, Somnath. 1981. *Kautilya and the Arthasastra*. New Delhi: Marwah Publications.

*Dharmasūtras: The Law Codes of Ancient India.* 1999. Edited and translated by Patrick Olivelle. New York: Oxford University Press.

Dikshitar, V. R. Ramachandra. 1927. "Kautalya and Machiavelli." *Indian Historical Quarterly* vol. 3, nos. 1-2, March: 176-80.

———. 1987 [1948]. *War in Ancient India*. 2nd ed. Delhi: Motilal Banarsidass.

———. 1993 [1932]. *The Mauryan Polity*. Delhi: Motilal Banarsidass.

Drekmeier, Charles. 1962. *Kingship and Community in Early India*. Stanford: Stanford University Press.

Dumont, Louis. 1962. "The Concept of Kingship in Ancient India." *Contributions to Indian Sociology* vol. 6, no. 1: 47-77.

Eliade, Mircea. 1992. "Time and Eternity in Indian Thought," in Prasad, Hari Shankar, ed. *Time in Indian Philosophy: A Collection of Essays*. Delhi: Sri Satguru Publications: 97-124.

Embree, Ainslie T., ed. 1988. *Sources of Indian Tradition: Volume One, from the Beginning to 1800*. 2nd rev. ed. New York: Columbia University Press.

Flood, Gavin. 1996. *An Introduction to Hinduism*. Cambridge, Eng.: Cambridge University Press.

Frauwallner, Erich. 1993 [1973]. *History of Indian Philosophy*. 2 vols. Delhi: Motilal Banarsidass.

Galey, Jean-Claude. 1989. "Reconsidering Kingship in India." *History and Anthropology* vol. 4, n.n., September: 123-87.

Ganguly, D. K. 1994. *Ancient India: History and Archaeology*. New Delhi: Abhinav Publications.

Ghosh, A. 1973. *The City in Early Historical India*. Simla, India: Indian Institute of Advanced Study.

Ghosh, Shyam. 1989. *Hindu Concept of Life and Death*. New Delhi: Munshiram Manoharlal.

Ghoshal, U. 1923. *A History of Hindu Political Theories*. London: Oxford University Press.

———. 1952. "The Authority of the King in Kautilya's Political Thought." *Indian Historical Quarterly* vol. 28, no. 4, December: 307-11.

———. 1996. "Industry, Trade, and Currency," in Sastri, K. A. Nilakanta, ed. *Age of the Nandas and Mauryas*. 2nd ed. Delhi: Motilal Banarsidass: 259-84.

Gonda, J. 1956. "Ancient Indian Kingship from the Religious Point of View." *Numen* vol. 3, n.n.: 36-71 and 122-55.

Goodall, Dominic, ed. 1996. *Hindu Scriptures*. Translated by Dominic Goodall. Berkeley: University of California Press.

Goswami, Mathura Nath. 1994. *Kautilya to Gandhi: A Study in the Philosophy of History*. Guwati, India: Bani Prokash.

Harvey, Peter. 1990. *An Introduction to Buddhism: Teachings, History and Practices*. Cambridge, Eng.: Cambridge University Press.

Heesterman, J. C. 1986. "The King's Order." *Contributions to Indian Sociology* vol. 20, no. 1: 1-13.

Hobbes, Thomas. 1988 [1651]. *Leviathan*. London: Penguin Books.

Hopkins, Thomas J. 1971. *The Hindu Religious Tradition*. Belmont, California: Wadsworth.

*The Holy Bible*. 1962. Revised Standard Version. New York: The World Publishing Company.

Indra. 1957. *Ideologies of War and Peace in Ancient India*. Hoshiarpur, India: Vishveshvaranand Institute Publications.

Jackson, Robert, and Georg Sørensen. 1999. *Introduction to International Relations*. Oxford, Eng.: Oxford University Press.

Jha, Vivekanand. 1991. "Social Stratification in Ancient India: Some Reflections." *Social Scientist* vol. 19, nos. 3-4, March: 19-40.

Johnson, Laurie M. 1993. *Thucydides, Hobbes, and the Interpretation of Realism*. Dekalb: Northern Illinois University Press.

Kangle, R. P. 1992 [1965]. *The Kautilīya Arthaśāstra*, Part III, *A Study*. Delhi: Motilal Banardisass.

Kautilya. 1992 [300 B.C.E.?] *The Arthashastra*, 2nd ed., edited and translated by R. P. Kangle, Part II of *The Kautilīya Arthaśāstra*. Delhi: Motilal Banardisass.

Keegan, John. 1993. *A History of Warfare*. New York: Alfred A. Knopf.

Kennedy, Richard S. 1976. "The King in Early South India, as Chieftain and Emperor." *Indian Historical Review* vol. 3, no. 1: 1-15.

Kirk, William. 1978. "Town and Country Planning in Ancient India According to Kautilya's *Arthashastra*." *Scottish Geographical Magazine* vol. 94, no. 2: 67-75.

Kohli, Ritu. 1995. *Kautilya's Political Theory: Yogakshema—The Concept of the Welfare State*. New Delhi: Deep & Deep.

Kosambi, D. D. 1994 [1964]. *The Culture and Civilisation of Ancient India*. Delhi: Vikas Publishing House.

Krishna, Daya. 1996. *The Problematic and Conceptual Structure of Classical Indian Thought About Man, Society and Polity*. Delhi: Oxford University Press.

Kulke, Hermann, and Dietmar Rothermund. 1991. *A History of India*. New Delhi: Rupa & Co.

Lal, Deepak. 1988. *The Hindu Equilibrium, Volume I, Cultural Stability and Economic Stagnation*. Oxford: Clarendon Press.

Lannoy, Richard. 1992. "The Terror of Time," in Prasad, Hari Shankar, ed. *Time in Indian Philosophy: A Collection of Essays*. Delhi: Sri Satguru Publications: 415-22.

Law, N. N. 1914. *Studies in Ancient Hindu Polity*. Bombay, India: Longmans, Green and Co.

———. 1931a. "Dvaidhibhava in the Kautilīya." *Indian Historical Quarterly* vol. 7, n.n.: 253-58.

———. 1931b. "Studies in Kautilya." *Indian Historical Quarterly* vol. 7, n.n.: 464-74 and 709-15.

———. 1932. "Studies in Kautilya." *Indian Historical Quarterly* vol. 8, n.n.: 54-63.

*The Laws of Manu*. 1991. Edited and translated by Wendy Doniger and Brian K. Smith. London: Penguin Books.

Lipner, Julius. 1994. *Hindus: Their Religious Beliefs and Practices*. London: Routledge.

Machiavelli, Niccolò. 1965. *The Art of War*, in *The Chief Works and Others*, 3 vols., edited and translated by Allan Gilbert. Durham, N. C.: Duke University Press, vol. 2, 561-726.

———. 1950. *The Prince and The Discourses*. Translated by Luigi Ricci, E. R. P. Vincent, and Christian E. Detmold. New York: Modern Library.

*The Mahābhārata*. 1987. Retold by R. K. Narayan. New Delhi: Vision Books.

Mahapatra, L K. 1995. "Kingship in India and Southeast Asia: A Field of Transcultural Interaction." *Journal of the Indian Anthropological Society* vol. 30, no. 3, November: 201-15.

Majumdar, Bimal Kanti. 1960. *The Military System in Ancient India*. Calcutta: Firma K. L. Mukhopadhyay.

Malkini, G. R. 1992. "The Temporal and the Eternal," in Prasad, Hari Shankar, ed. *Time in Indian Philosophy: A Collection of Essays*. Delhi: Sri Satguru Publications, 699-707.

McCrindle, J. W. 1960. *Ancient India as Described by Megasthenes and*

*Arrian*. 2nd rev. ed. Calcutta: Chuckervertty Chatterjee & Co.

Mehta, Usha, and Usha Thakkar. 1980. *Kautilya and His Arthashastra*. New Delhi: S. Chand & Company.

Mishra, Bambahadur. 1965. *Polity in the Agni Purāna*. Calcutta: Punthi Pustak.

Mookerji, Radha Kumud. 1988. [1966]. *Chandragupta Maurya and His Times*. 4th ed. Delhi: Motilal Banarsidass.

Morgenthau, Hans. 1985. *Politics Among Nations: The Struggle for Power and Peace*. 6th ed. New York: Knopf.

Nag, Kalidas, and V. R. Ramachandra Dikshitar. 1927. "The Diplomatic Theories of Ancient India and the *Arthashastra*." *Journal of Indian History* vol. 6, no. 1: 15-35.

Nagarajan, V. 1992. *Evolution of Social Polity of Ancient India from Manu to Kautilya*, 2 vols. Nagpur, India: Dattsons.

Nigam, Shyamsunder. 1975. *Economic* Organisation in Ancient India: (200 BC—200 AD). New Delhi: Munshiram Manohariat.

Olivelle, Patrick. 1998. "Caste and Purity: A Study in the Language of the Dharma Literature." *Contributions to Indian Sociology* vol. 32, no. 2: 189-216.

Orwin, Clifford. 1994. *The Humanity of Thucydides*. Princeton: Princeton University Press.

Pande, G. C. 1984. *Foundations of Indian Culture: Spiritual Vision and Symbolic Forms in Ancient India*. New Delhi: Books & Books.

Panikkar, Raimundo. 1992. "Time and History in the Tradition of India: Kala and Karma," in Prasad, Hari Shankar, ed. *Time in Indian Philosophy: A Collection of Essays*. Delhi: Sri Satguru Publications: 21-46.

Perrett, Roy. W. 1998. *Hindu Ethics: A Philosophical Study*. Honolulu: University of Hawaii Press.

———. 1999. "History, Time, and Knowledge in Ancient India." *History and Theory* vol. 38, no. 3: 307-21.

Plato. 1961. *The Republic*, trans. Paul Shorey, in Hamilton, Edith, ed. *The Collected Dialogues of Plato*. Princeton: Princeton University Press.

———. 1961. *Phaedrus*, trans. R. Hackforth, in Hamilton, Edith, ed. *The Collected Dialogues of Plato*. Princeton: Princeton University Press.

Prasad, Hari Shankar, ed. 1992. *Time in Indian Philosophy: A Collection of Essays*. Delhi: Sri Satguru Publications.

———. 1992. "The Problem of Time in Indian Philosophy: An Introduction," in Prasad, Hari Shankar, ed. *Time in Indian Philosophy: A Collection of Essays*. Delhi: Sri Satguru Publications: 1-20.

Prasad, Rajendra. 1989. *Politico-Geographical Analysis of the Arthashastra*.

New Delhi: Inter-India Publications.

Puligandla, R. 1992. "Time and History in the Indian Tradition," in Prasad, Hari Shankar, ed. *Time in Indian Philosophy: A Collection of Essays*. Delhi: Sri Satguru Publications: 409-14.

Rahula, Walpola. 1974. *What the Buddha Taught*. 2nd rev. ed. New York: Grove Press.

Rai, Kauleshawr. 1992. *Ancient India*. Allahabad, India: Kitab Mahal.

Ramaswamy, T. N. 1994 [1962]. *Essentials of Indian Statecraft: Kautilya's Arthashastra for Contemporary Readers*. New Delhi: Munshiram Manoharlal.

*The Rāmāyana*. 1977. Retold by R. K. Narayan. New York: Penguin Books.

Rangarajan, L. N. 1992. *The Arthashastra*. Edited and translated by L. N. Rangarajan. New Delhi: Penguin Books.

Rao, M. V. Krishna. 1958. *Studies in Kautilya*. 2nd ed. New Delhi: Munshi Ram Manohar Lal.

Raychaudhuri, H. C. 1996a. "India in the Age of the Nandas," in Sastri, K. A. Nilakanta, ed. *Age of the Nandas and Mauryas*. 2nd ed. Delhi: Motilal Banarsidass: 9- 45.

———. 1996b. "Chandragupta and Bindusara," in Sastri, K. A. Nilakanta, ed. *Age of the Nandas and Mauryas*. 2nd ed. Delhi: Motilal Banarsidass: 132-70.

Rhys Davids, T. W. 1993. [1903]. *Buddhist India*. Delhi: Motilal Banarsidass.

*The Rig Veda*. Edited and translated by Wendy Doniger O'Flaherty. Baltimore, Md.: Penguin Books.

Riley, Jack. 2000. "Freedom and Empire: The Politics of Athenian Imperialism," in Gustafson, Lowell S., ed. *Thucydides' Theory of International Relations: A Lasting Possession*. Baton Rouge: Lousiana State University Press, 117-50

Robinson, John Mansley. 1968. *An Introduction to Early Greek Philosophy*. New York: Houghton Mifflin Company.

Rocher, Ludo. 1986. *The Purānas*. Wiesbaden, Ger.: Otto Harrassowitz.

Roy, Somendra Lal. 1992. "Kautilya's Concept of State." *Socialist Perspective* vol. 20, nos. 1-2, June-September: 93-99.

Saletore, Bhasker Anand. 1963. *Ancient Indian Political Thought and Institutions*. London: Asia Publishing House.

Saletore, R. N. 1975. *Early Indian Economic History*. London: Curzon Press.

Samozvantsev, A. M. 1984. "Some Remarks on the Land Relations in *The Kautilīya Arthaśāstra*." *Indo-Iranian Journal* vol. 27, n. n.: 275-89.

Sarkar, Benoy Kumar. 1935. "Kautalya: Economic Planning and Climatology." *Indian Historical Quarterly* vol. 11, no. 2, June: 328-50.

Sarma, Nataraja. 1991. "Measures of Time in Ancient India." *Endeavor* vol. 15, no. 4: 185-88.

Sastri, K. A. Nilakanta, ed. 1996a [1967] *Age of the Nandas and Mauryas.* 2nd ed. Delhi: Motilal Banarsidass.

———. 1996b. "Alexander's Campaigns in India," in Sastri, K. A. Nilakanta, ed. *Age of the Nandas and Mauryas.* 2nd ed. Delhi: Motilal Banarsidass: 46-80.

———. 1996c. "Aśoka and His Successors," in Sastri, K. A. Nilakanta, ed. *Age of the Nandas and Mauryas.* 2nd ed. Delhi: Motilal Banarsidass: 202-48.

———. 1996d. "India in Early Greek and Latin Literature," in Sastri, K. A. Nilakanta, ed. *Age of the Nandas and Mauryas.* 2nd ed. Delhi: Motilal Banarsidass: 81-122.

———. 1996e. "Mauryan Polity," in Sastri, K. A. Nilakanta, ed. *Age of the Nandas and Mauryas.* 2nd ed. Delhi: Motilal Banarsidass: 171-201.

Selvanayagam, Israel. 1992. "Aśoka and Arjuna as Counter-Figures Standing on the Field of Dharma: A Historical-Hermeneutical Perspective." *History of Religions* vol. 32, no. 1: 59-75.

Sen, Benoy Chandra. 1967. *Economics in Kautilya.* Calcutta: Sanskrit College.

Sen, Raj Kumar. 1990. "Taxation Principles During Kautilya's Age." *Indian Economic Journal* vol. 37, no. 4, April: 133-38.

Sharma, Arvind. 2000. *Classical Hindu Thought: An Introduction.* Oxford, Eng.: Oxford University Press.

Sharma, Manjusha. 1987. "Organizational Structure of Justice in the *Arthashastra.*" *Vishveshvaranand Indological Journal* vol. 25, no. 1: 121-29.

Sharma, Ram Sharan. 1954. "Superstition and Politics in the *Arthashastra* of Kautilya." *Journal of the Bihar Research Society* vol. 40, no. 3: 223-31.

———. 1990. *Sudras in Ancient India.* 3rd rev. ed. Delhi: Motilal Banarsidass.

———. 1991. *Aspects of Political Ideas and Institutions in Ancient India.* 3rd rev. ed. Delhi: Motilal Banarsidass.

Shastri, Shakuntala Rao. 1969. *Women in the Vedic Age.* 4th ed. Bombay, India: Bharatiya Vidya Bhavan.

Sil, Narasingha Prosad. 1984. "Kautilya's *Arthashastra* and Machiavellism: A Reevaluation." *Quarterly Review of Historical Studies* (Nigeria) vol. 23, no. 2: 10-23.

———. 1985. "Political Morality vs. Political Necessity: Kautilya and

Machiavelli Revisited." *Journal of Asian History* vol. 19, no. 2: 101- 42.

———. 1989. *Kautilya's Arthashastra: A Comparative Study.* New York: Peter Lang.

Sinari, Ramakant A. 1984. *The Structure of Indian Thought.* Delhi: Oxford University Press.

Singh, G. P. 1993. *Political Thought in Ancient India.* New Delhi: D. K. Printworld.

Singh, Satya Narain. 1992. *Political Ideas and Institutions Under the Mauryas.* Patna, India: Janaki Prakashan.

Smith, Brian K. 1994. *Classifying the Universe: The Ancient Indian Varna System and the Origins of Caste.* New York: Oxford University Press.

Spellman, John W. 1964. *Political Theory of Ancient India.* Oxford, Eng.: Oxford University Press.

Srivastava, Arvind Kumar. 1985. *The Ancient Indian Army: Its Administration and Organization.* Delhi: Ajanta Publications.

Stein, Burton. 1998. *A History of India.* Oxford, Eng.: Blackwell Publishers.

Strong, John S. 1995. *The Experience of Buddhism: Sources and Interpretations.* Belmont, Calif.: Wadsworth.

Subramaniam, V. 1998. "The Administrative Legacy of Ancient India." *International Journal of Public Administration* vol. 21, no. 1: 87-108.

Sun Tzu. 1963. *The Art of War.* Translated by Samuel B. Griffith. London: Oxford University Press.

Thapar, Romila. 1966. *A History of India.* Baltimore, Md.: Penguin Books.

———. 1978. *Ancient Indian Social History: Some Interpretations.* New Delhi: Orient Longman.

———. 1987. *The Mauryas Revisited.* Calcutta: K. P. Bagchi & Company.

———. 1992. *Interpreting Early India.* Delhi: Oxford University Press.

———. 1997. *Aśoka and the Decline of the Mauryas.* Delhi: Oxford University Press.

Thomas, P. 1964. *Indian Women Through the Ages.* Bombay, India: Asia Publishing House.

Thucydides. 1972. *History of the Peloponnesian War.* Translated by Rex Warner. Baltimore, Md.: Penguin Books.

*The Upanishads.* 1965. Edited and translated by Juan Mascaro. London: Penguin Books.

Vigasin, A. A. and A. M. Samozvantsev. 1985. *Society, State and Law in Ancient India.* New Delhi: Sterling Publishers.

Waltz, Kenneth. 1979. *Theory of International Relations.* New York: McGraw-Hill.

Weber, Max. 1919. "Politics as a Vocation," 212-25 in 1978, *Weber:*

*Selections in Translation.* Edited by W. G. Runciman, translated by Eric Matthews. Cambridge, Eng.: Cambridge University Press.

Wolpert, Stanley. 1982. *A New History of India.* 2nd ed. New York: Oxford University Press.

Zaehner, R.C. 1966. *Hinduism.* 2nd ed. Oxford, Eng.: Oxford University Press.

Zimmer, Heinrich. 1967. *Philosophies of India.* Princeton: Princeton University Press.

# Index

# About the Author

Roger Boesche received his Ph.D. in political science from Stanford University, and he has taught the history of political thought at Occidental College in Los Angeles since 1977. He is Professor of Politics and The Arthur G. Coons Professor of the History of Ideas at Occidental. He has published numerous articles and the following books: *Alexis de Tocqueville: Selected Letters on Politics and Society* (University of California Press, 1985); *The Strange Liberalism of Alexis de Tocqueville* (Cornell University Press, 1987); and *Theories of Tyranny: From Plato to Arendt* (Penn State University Press, 1996). He received his second National Endowment for the Humanities Fellowship in order to complete the research and writing of this book on Kautilya. He lives in Los Angeles with his wife Mandy, his daughter Kelsey, and many good friends.